Internet in an Hour for Sales People

Chris Katsaropoulos

Don Mayo

Kathy Berkemeyer

Acknowledgements

To my father, John Katsaropoulos, for teaching me how to learn.
A special thanks to Jennifer Frew, Peter McCarthy, and John Visaggi at DDC Publishing for always listening and knowing the right thing to do.

Chris Katsaropoulos

To Jen for her double-duty efforts as Major Domo of the sanity patrol, Lisa Miller for always being available to help and laugh, and Marivel for her unconditional encouragement. *Don Mayo*

Dedicated to the memory of my parents, John and Gert Madden.

Kathy Berkemeyer

Managing Editor	Technical Editors	English Editors	Illustrations	Design and Layout
Jennifer Frew	Monique Peterson Cathy Vesecky	Jennifer Frew Monique Peterson	Ryan Sather	Elsa Johannesson Midori Nakamura Paul Wray

ISBN: 1-56243-604-X
Cat. No. HR4
First DDC Publishing, Inc. Printing:
10 9 8 7 6 5 4 3 2 1
Printed in the United States of America.

Contents

Contents

Introduction

This Book is Designed for You . . .

if you are a busy sales representative, sales manager, staff member, or small business owner who wants to find out how to close more sales using the Internet.

The Internet and especially the World Wide Web provide a vast and ever-growing resource where you can find information and sales tools to help you improve your sales revenue. This book shows you where and how to find the best resources available.

This book has two main sections, Internet Basics and Web Resources.

Internet Basics

In Internet Basics, you can learn how to:

- Use Netscape Navigator to browse the World Wide.
- Send and receive e-mail messages with Netscape Messenger.
- Use Internet Explorer to browse the World Wide Web.
- Send and receive e-mail messages with Microsoft Outlook Express.
- Access the Internet using America Online.
- Send and receive e-mail messages with America Online.
- Find information on the Web with search engines.

Web Resources

Web Resources shows you ways you can use the Web to do your job more effectively.

Web Resources is organized by general categories (such as Prospecting, Closing the Sale, and Saving Money), then by topics (such as Improve Sales Techniques, Market Your Product on the Web, Develop Direct Marketing Online, and Research a Target Market).

Each topic showcases top Web sites that offer practical business resources. Each Web site listing provides you with the site's URL (Web address) and a brief description of how the site can help you. In many cases an illustration of the web site is also provided.

Appendices

These Appendices give you additional reference information about the following topics:

Essential Downloads
A listing of Web sites where you can download useful software, much of it available free of charge or for a minimal registration fee.

Timesaving Tools
Use these sites to get quick answers and information.

Emoticons and Abbreviations
Symbols and abbreviations used when communicating electronically.

Netiquette
A guide to using "net etiquette" when communicating and browsing online.

Viruses
An overview of what computers viruses can do to your computer and how to avoid them.

Glossary
A listing of Internet and World Wide Web terminology complete with definitions.

What Do I Need to Use This Book

This book assumes that you have some general knowledge and experience with computers, and that you already know how to perform the following tasks:

- Use a mouse (double-click, etc.).
- Make your way around Microsoft Windows 95.
- Install and run programs.

If you are completely new to computers as well as the World Wide Web, you may want to refer to DDC's **Learning Microsoft Windows 95** or **Learning the Internet**.

This book also assumes that you have access to browser applications such as Microsoft Internet Explorer 4.0, Netscape Navigator 4.0, or America Online.

√ *If you do not currently have these applications, contact your Internet Service Provider for instructions on how to download them. You can also use other browsers or previous versions such as Explorer 3.0 and Navigator 3.0 to browse the Web.*

You must have an Internet connection, either through your school, your office, or an online service such as America OnLine or Compuserve. How to get connected to the Internet is not covered in this book.

Please read over the following list of "must haves" to ensure that you are ready to be connected to the Internet.

- A computer (with a recommended minimum of 16 MB of RAM) and a modem port.

- A modem (with a recommended minimum speed of 14.4kbps, and suggested speed of 28.8kbps) that is connected to an analog phone line (assuming you are not using a direct Internet connection through a school, corporation, etc.).

- Established access to the Internet through an online service, independent Internet service provider, etc.

- A great deal of patience. The Internet is a fun and exciting place. But getting connected can be frustrating at times. Expect to run into occasional glitches, to get disconnected from time to time, and to experience occasional difficulty in viewing certain web pages or features. The more up-to-date your equipment and software are, however, the less difficulty you will probably experience.

Internet Cautions

ACCURACY: Be cautious not to believe everything on the Internet. Almost anyone can publish information on the Internet, and since there is no Internet editor or monitor, some information may be false. All information found on the World Wide Web should be checked for accuracy through additional reputable sources.

SECURITY: When sending information over the Internet, be prepared to let the world have access to it. Computer hackers can find ways to access anything that you send to anyone over the Internet, including e-mail. Be cautious when sending confidential information to anyone.

VIRUSES: These small, usually destructive computer programs hide inside of innocent-looking programs. Once a virus is executed, it attaches itself to other programs. When triggered, often by the occurrence of a date or time on the computer's internal clock/calendar, it executes a nuisance or damaging function, such as displaying a message on your screen, corrupting your files, or reformatting your hard disk.

BASICS

Netscape Navigator: 1

◆ About Netscape Navigator ◆ Start Netscape Navigator
◆ The Netscape Screen ◆ Exit Netscape Navigator

About Netscape Navigator

- Netscape Navigator 4.0 is the Internet browser component of Netscape Communicator, a set of integrated tools for browsing the World Wide Web, finding and downloading information, shopping for and purchasing goods and services, creating Web pages, and communicating with others with e-mail. This chapter focuses on the Netscape Navigator browser. Netscape Messenger, the e-mail component, is covered in Chapters 4-6.

Start Netscape Navigator

To start Netscape Navigator (Windows 95):

- Click the Start button 📶 Start.

- Click Programs, Netscape Communicator, Netscape Navigator.

  OR

- If you have a shortcut to Netscape Communicator 🗔 on your desktop, double-click it to start Netscape Navigator.

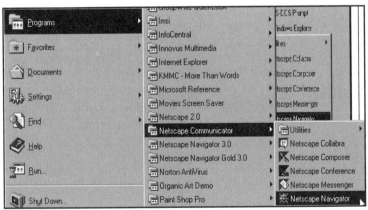

√ The first time you start Netscape Communicator, the New Profile Setup dialog box appears. Enter information about your e-mail name and service provider in the dialog boxes that appear. If you do not know the information, you can leave it blank until you are ready to fill it in.

The Netscape Screen

■ The Netscape Navigator screen contains features that will be very helpful as you explore the Internet. Some of these features are constant and some change depending on the Web site visited or the task attempted or completed.

√ *To gain more space on screen, you may want to hide toolbars and the Location line. Go to the View menu and select the desired hide/show options.*

Title bar   Displays the name of the program (Netscape) and the current Web page (Welcome to Netscape). Note the standard Windows minimize, maximize/restore, and close buttons at the right.

Menu bar   Displays menus, which provide drop-down lists of commands for executing Netscape tasks.

Navigation toolbar   Contains buttons for moving between and printing Web pages. The name and icon on each button identify the command for the button. You can access these commands quickly and easily by clicking the mouse on the desired button.

If the toolbar buttons are not visible, open the View menu and click Show Navigation Toolbar.

Location toolbar   Displays the electronic address of the currently displayed Web page in the Location field. You can also type the electronic address of a Web page in the Location field and press Enter to access it. A Web site address is called a Uniform Resource Locator (URL).

If the Location toolbar is not visible, open the View menu and click Show Location Toolbar.

 The Location toolbar also contains the Bookmarks QuickFile button. Click this button to view a list of sites that you have bookmarked for quick access. (For more information on bookmarks, see "Netscape Navigator: 3" on page 9.)

 The Location button is also located on this toolbar. The word *Netsite* displays if the current Web site uses Netscape software. The word *Location* replaces Netsite if the site does not use Netscape as its primary software.

Personal toolbar

Contains buttons or links that you add to connect to your favorite sites. When you install Netscape Communicator, the Internet, Lookup, New&Cool, and Netcaster buttons are on the Personal toolbar by default. You can delete these buttons and add your own by displaying the desired Web site and dragging the Location icon onto the Personal toolbar.

Netscape's status indicator

Netscape's icon  pulses when Netscape is processing a request (command) that you enter. To return immediately to Netscape's home page, click on this icon.

Status bar

When a Web page is opening, the Status bar indicates progress by a percentage displayed in the center and the security level of the page being loaded by a lock in the far-left corner. When you place the cursor over a hyperlink, the Status bar displays the URL of the link.

Component toolbar

The buttons on this toolbar are links to other Communicator components: Navigator, (Messenger) Mailbox, (Collabra) Discussions, and (Page) Composer.

Exit Netscape Navigator

■ Exiting Netscape Navigator and disconnecting from your Internet Service Provider (ISP) are two separate steps. You can actually disconnect from your service provider and still have Netscape Navigator open. (Remember that you must first establish a connection to the Internet via your ISP to use Netscape to access information on the Web.) You can also disconnect from Navigator and still have your ISP open.

■ There are times when you may want to keep Netscape open to read information obtained from the Web, access information stored on your hard disk using Netscape, or to compose e-mail to send later. If you don't disconnect from your ISP and you pay an hourly rate, you will continue incurring charges.

> **CAUTION** When you exit Netscape, you do not necessarily exit from your Internet service provider. Be sure to check the disconnect procedure from your ISP so that you will not continue to be charged for time online. Most services disconnect when a certain amount of time passes with no activity.

√ *Once you disconnect from your ISP, you can no longer access new Web information. Remember: Netscape Navigator is a browser; it is not an Internet connection.*

√ *You can disconnect from your ISP and view Web information accessed during the current session using the Back and Forward toolbar buttons. This is because the visited sites are stored in the memory of your computer. However, Web sites visited during the current session are erased from your computer memory when you exit Netscape.*

Netscape Navigator: 2

The Navigation Toolbar

- The Netscape Navigation toolbar displays buttons for Netscape's most commonly used commands. Note that each button contains an icon and a word describing the button's function. Choosing any of these buttons activates the indicated task immediately.

- If the Navigation toolbar is not visible, select Show Navigation Toolbar from the View menu.

 Moves back through pages previously displayed. Back is available only if you have moved around among Web pages in the current Navigator session; otherwise, it is dimmed.

 Moves forward through pages previously displayed. Forward is available only if you have used the Back button; otherwise, it is dimmed.

 Reloads the currently displayed Web page. Use this button if the current page is taking too long to display or to update the current page with any changes that may have been made since the page was downloaded.

 Displays the home page.

 Displays Netscape's Net Search Page. You can select one of several search tools from this page.

 Displays a menu with helpful links to Internet sites that contain search tools and services.

 Prints the displayed page, topic, or article.

 Displays security information for the displayed Web page as well as information on Netscape security features.

Stops the loading of a Web page.

URLs (Uniform Resource Locator)

■ Every Web site has a unique address called its URL (Uniform Resource Locator). A URL has four parts:

Part	Example	Description
Protocol	**http://**	The protocol indicates the method used for communicating on the internet The most common is http:// , which stands for Hypertext Transfer Protocol. Another protocol—ftp:// (file transfer protocol)—is used with internet sites designed to make files available for uploading and downloading.
Address type	**www.**	www. stands for World Wide Web and indicates that the site is located on the Web. Occasionally, you may find other address types, but www. addresses are the most common.
Identifier of the site's owner	**ddcpub**	This part of the address identifies who is responsible for the Web site.
Domain	**.com, .gov, .org, .edu, etc.** (see below)	The domain indicates the kind of organization that sponsors the site (company, government, non-profit organization, educational institution, and so on).

■ For example, the DDC publishing URL breaks down as follows:

http://www.ddcpub.com

Hypertext Transfer Protocol　　World Wide Web　　Company name　　Domain

■ There are seven common domains:

com	Commercial enterprise	**edu**	Educational institution
org	Non-commercial organization	**mil**	U. S. Military location
net	A network that has a gateway to the Internet	**gov**	Local, state, or federal government location
int	International organization		

Open World Wide Web Sites

- There are several ways to access a Web site. If you know the site's address, you can enter the correct Web address (URL) on the Location field on the Location toolbar.

- If the address you are entering is the address of a site you have visited recently or that you have bookmarked (see "Netscape Navigator: 3" on page 9 for more information on Bookmarks), you will notice as you begin to type the address that Netscape attempts to complete it for you. If the address that Netscape suggests is the one you want, press Enter.

- If the address that Netscape suggests is not correct, keep typing to complete the desired address and then press Enter. Or, you can click the down arrow next to the Location field to view a list of other possible matches, select an address, and press Enter.

- You can also enter the URL in the Open Page dialog box. To do so, select Open Page from the File menu, select Navigator, type the URL, and click Open.

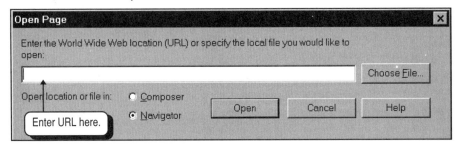

- There are a couple of shortcuts for entering URL addresses. One shortcut involves omitting the http://www. prefix from the Web address. Netscape assumes the **http://** protocol and the **www** that indicates that the site is located on the Web. If you are trying to connect to a company Web site, entering the company name is generally sufficient. Netscape assumes the **.com** suffix. For example, entering **ddcpub** on the location line and pressing Enter would reach the **http://www.ddcpub.com** address.

  √ *Don't be discouraged if the connection to the World Wide Web site is not made immediately. The site may be off-line temporarily. The site may also be very busy with others users trying to access it. Be sure the URL is typed accurately. Occasionally, it takes several tries to connect to a site.*

Netscape Navigator: 3

◆ History List ◆ Bookmarks ◆ Add Bookmarks
◆ Delete Bookmarks ◆ Print Web Pages

History List

- While you move back and forth among Web sites, Netscape automatically records each of these site locations in a **history** list, which is temporarily stored on your computer. You can use the history list to track what sites you have already visited or to jump to a recently viewed site.

  √ *As you move from one site to another on the Web, you may find yourself asking, "How did I get here?" The History list is an easy way to see the path you followed to get to the current destination.*

- To view the history list, click <u>H</u>istory on the <u>C</u>ommunicator menu, or press Ctrl+H. To link to a site shown in the history list, double-click on it.

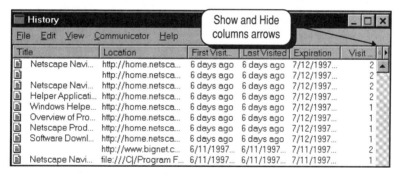

Bookmarks

- A **bookmark** is a placeholder containing the title and URL of a Web page that, when selected, links directly to that page. If you find a Web site that you like and want to revisit, you can create a bookmark to record its location. (See "Add Bookmarks" on page 10.) The Netscape bookmark feature maintains permanent records of the Web sites in your bookmark files so that you can return to them easily.

- You can view the Bookmarks menu by selecting <u>B</u>ookmarks from the <u>C</u>ommunicator menu or by clicking on the Bookmarks QuickFile button 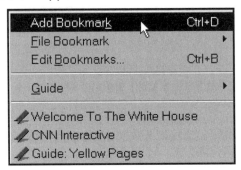 on the Location toolbar. The drop-down menu shown below appears.

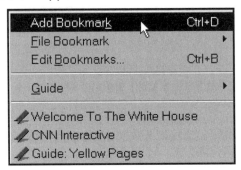

Add Bookmarks

- Display the Web page to add, go to <u>B</u>ookmarks on the <u>C</u>ommunicator menu and click Add Bookmar<u>k</u>.

Netscape does not confirm that a bookmark has been added to the file.

- You can create bookmarks from addresses in the History folder. Click <u>C</u>ommunicator, <u>H</u>istory and select the listing to bookmark. Right-click on it and choose Add To Bookmar<u>k</u>s from the menu.

Delete Bookmarks

- Bookmarks may be deleted at anytime. For example, you may wish to delete a bookmark if a Web site no longer exists or remove one that is no longer of interest to you.
- To delete a bookmark do the following:
  - Click <u>C</u>ommunicator.
  - Click <u>B</u>ookmarks.
  - Click Edit <u>B</u>ookmarks.
  - In the Bookmarks window, select the bookmark you want to delete by clicking on it from the bookmark list.
  - Press the Delete key.

10

OR

- Right-click on the bookmark and select Delete Bookmark from the drop-down menu.

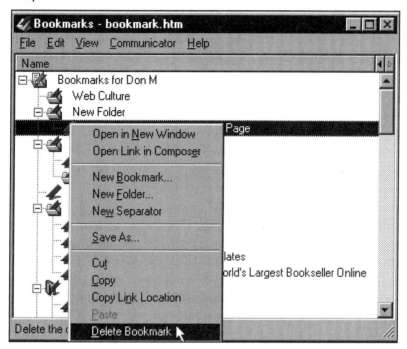

Print Web Pages

- One of the many uses of the Internet is to print out information. You can print a page as it appears on screen, or you can print it as plain text. Only displayed pages can be printed.
- To print a Web page, display it and do the following:

  - Click the Print button [Print] on the Navigation toolbar.

    OR

  - Click Print on the File menu.

  - In the Print dialog box that displays, select the desired print options and click Print.

- In most cases, the Web page will be printed in the format shown in the Web page display.

Netscape Messenger: 4

◆ **Configure Netscape Mail** ◆ **Start Netscape Messenger**
◆ **The Message List Window** ◆ **Get New Mail** ◆ **Read Messages**
◆ **Delete a Message** ◆ **Print Messages** ◆ **Bookmark a Message**

Configure Netscape Mail

√ *This section assumes that you have already set up an e-mail account with a service provider. If you do not have an e-mail address, contact your Internet Service Provider. Establishing a modem connection and configuring your computer to send and receive mail can be frustrating. Don't be discouraged; what follows are steps that will get you connected, but some of the information may have to be supplied by your Internet Service Provider. Calling for help will save you time and frustration.*

■ The Netscape Communicator browser suite includes a comprehensive e-mail program called Netscape Messenger, which allows you to send, receive, save, and print e-mail messages and attachments.

■ Before you can use Messenger to send and receive e-mail, you must configure the program with your e-mail account information (user name, e-mail address, and mail server names). You may have already filled in this information if you completed the New Profile Setup Wizard when you installed Netscape Communicator.

■ You may have configured Netscape Messenger to receive and send e-mail messages when you first installed the program. If not, follow these steps to get connected. You can also use these steps to update and change settings to your e-mail account.

Identity Settings

• Open the Edit menu on the Netscape Navigator or Netscape Messenger menu and select Preferences. Click Identity in the Mail & Groups Category list to and do the following:

Enter your name and e-mail address in the first two boxes. Enter any other optional information in the Identity dialog box.

12

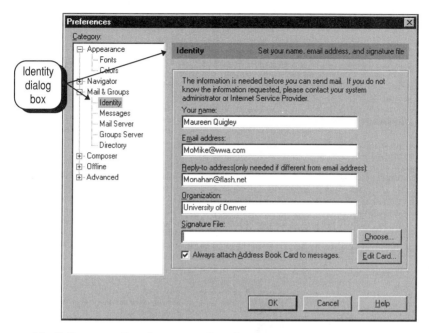

Mail Server Preference Settings

- Click Mail Server to configure your mailbox so that you can send and receive mail.

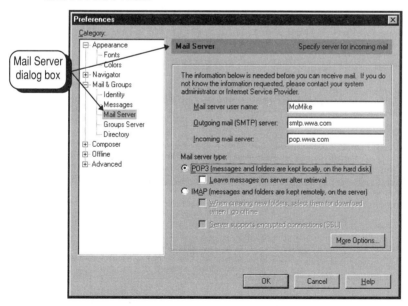

- Enter mail server user name in the first box. This is usually the part of your e-mail address that appears in front of the @ sign.

- Enter your outgoing and incoming mail server. Check with your Internet Service Provider if you are not sure what these settings are.

- Click OK to save and close the Preference settings. You should now be able to send and receive e-mail messages and/or files.

Start Netscape Messenger

■ To start Netscape Messenger:

- Click the Mailbox icon  on the Component bar.

  OR

- Start the Netscape Messenger program from the Netscape Communicator submenu on the Start menu.

The Message List Window

■ After you launch Messenger, a message list window will open, displaying the contents of the e-mail Inbox folder. You can retrieve, read, forward, and reply to messages from this window.

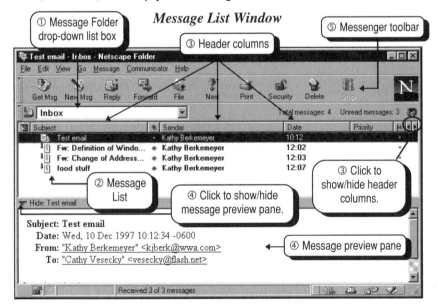

Message List Window

- The message list window includes the following:

① The **Message Folder drop-down list box** displays the currently selected message folder, the contents of which are displayed in the message list below the drop-down box. Click the down arrow to display a list of other message folders. Select a different folder from the list to display its contents in the message list area.

② The **message list** displays a header for each of the messages contained in the currently selected message folder (Inbox is the default).

③ **Header columns** list the categories of information available for each message, such as subject, sender, and date. You can customize the display of the header columns in a number of ways:

- Resize column widths by placing the mouse pointer over the right border of a column until the pointer changes to a double arrow, and then click and drag the border to the desired size.

- Rearrange the order of the columns by clicking and dragging a header to a new location in the series.

- Show/hide different columns by clicking the arrow buttons on the upper-right side of the message list window.

  √   *If text in a message header is cut off so that you cannot read it all, position the mouse pointer on the header in the column containing the cropped text. A small box will display the complete text for that column of the header, as in the example below:*

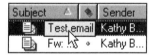

④ The **message preview pane** displays the content of the message currently selected from the message list. You can show/hide the preview pane by clicking on the blue triangle icon in the bottom-left corner of the message list pane. You can resize the preview pane or the message list pane by placing the pointer over the border between the two panes until the pointer changes to a double arrow and then dragging the border up or down to the desired size.

⑤ The **Messenger toolbar** displays buttons for activating Netscape Messenger's most commonly used commands. Note that each button contains an image and a word describing the function. Choosing any of these buttons will activate the indicated task immediately.

Messenger Toolbar Buttons and Functions

 Retrieves new mail from your Internet mail server and loads it into the Inbox message folder.

 Opens the Message Composition screen allowing you to compose new mail messages.

 Allows you to reply to the sender of an e-mail message or to the sender and all other recipients of the e-mail message.

 Forwards a message you have received to another address.

 Stores the current message in one of six Messenger default file folders or in a new folder that you create.

 Selects and displays the next of the unread messages in your Inbox.

 Prints the displayed message.

 Displays the security status of a message.

 Deletes the selected message. Deleted messages are moved to the Trash folder. You must delete contents of Trash folder to remove messages from your computer.

Get New Mail

- Since new e-mail messages are stored on a remote ISP mail server, you must be connected to the Internet to access them. To retrieve new messages to your computer, click the Get Msg button on the Messenger toolbar.

- In the Password Entry dialog box that follows, enter your e-mail password in the blank text box and click OK. (If you do not know your e-mail password, contact your ISP.)

16

√ *Messenger saves your password for the rest of the current Messenger session. You must re-enter it each time you retrieve new mail, unless you set Messenger to save your password permanently. To do so:*

- Click Edit, Preferences.

- Click once on Mail Server under Mail & Groups.

- Click the More Options button.

- Select the Remember my mail password check box and click OK twice.

■ The Getting New Messages box opens, displaying the status of your message retrieval.

■ Once your new messages are retrieved, they are listed in the message list window. By default, Messenger stores new mail messages in the Inbox folder.

Read Messages

■ You can read a message in the preview pane of the message list window or in a separate window.

■ To read a message in the preview pane, click on the desired message header in the message list. If the message does not appear, click on the blue triangle icon at the bottom of the message list window to display the preview pane.

■ To open and read a message in a separate window, double-click on the desired message header in the message list. You can close a message after reading it by clicking File, Close or by clicking on the Close button (X) in the upper-right corner of the window.

■ To read the next unread message, click the Next button on the Messenger toolbar. Or, if you have reached the end of the current message, you can press the spacebar to proceed to the next unread message.

- Once you have read a message, it remains stored in the Inbox folder until you delete it or file it in another folder. (See "Delete a Message" below.)

  √ *You do not have to be online to read e-mail. You can reduce your online charges if you disconnect from your ISP after retrieving your messages and read them offline.*

  √ *Icons located to the left of message headers in the message list identify each message as either unread ▭ (retrieved during a previous Messenger session), new ▭ (and unread), or read ▭.*

Delete a Message

- To delete a message, select its header from the message list window and click the Delete button ⟦ Delete ⟧ in the Messenger toolbar.

  √ *To select more than one message to delete, click the Ctrl button while you click each message header.*

Print Messages

- In order to print a message you must first display the message in either the preview pane of the message list window or in a separate window, then:

  - Click the Print button ⟦ Print ⟧ on the Messenger toolbar.

  - In the Print dialog box that appears, select the desired print options and click OK.

Print Dialog Box

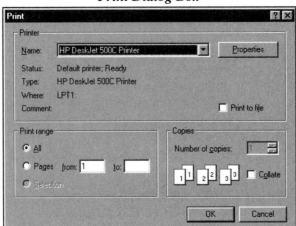

Bookmark a Message

- You can add an e-mail message to your Bookmarks folder for easy access from anywhere within the Communicator suite. To bookmark a message:

  - Display the message you want to bookmark in either the preview pane of the message list window or in a separate window.

  - Select Communicator, Bookmarks, Add Bookmark.

- Messenger will add the message to the bottom of your Bookmarks menu.

◆ **Compose New Messages** ◆ **Send Messages**
◆ **The Message Composition Toolbar** ◆ **Reply to Mail**
◆ **Forward Mail** ◆ **Add Entries to the Personal Address Book**
◆ **Address a New Message Using the Personal Address Book**

Compose New Messages

■ You can compose an e-mail message in Netscape Messenger while you are connected to the Internet, or while you are offline. When composing an e-mail message online, you can send the message immediately after creating it. When composing a message offline (which is considered proper Netiquette—net etiquette), you will need to store the message in your Unsent Messages folder until you are online and can send it.

■ To create a message, you first need to open Messenger's Message Composition window. To do so:

  • Click the New Message button New Msg .

    √ *The Message Composition window displays.*

Netscape Message Composition Window

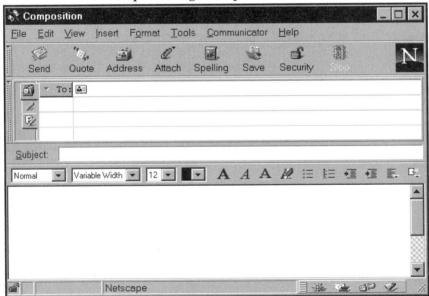

√ *You can hide any toolbar in the Message Composition screen by going to View, Hide Message Toolbar or Hide Formatting Toolbar.*

√ *If you do not know the recipient's address, you can look it up and insert it from your personal address book (see page 24) or an online directory.*

■ In the Message Composition window, type the Internet address(es) of the message recipient(s) in the To: field. Or, click the Address

button ▨ Address on the Message Composition toolbar and select an address to insert (see pages 24-26 for more information on using the Address Book).

√ *If you are sending the message to multiple recipients, press Enter after typing each recipient's address.*

■ After inserting the address(es), click the To: icon ▨ ▾ To: to display a drop-down menu of other addressee options. Select any of the following options from the drop-down menu and enter the recipient information indicated.

To	The e-mail address of the person to whom the message is being sent.
CC (Carbon Copy)	The e-mail addresses of people who will receive copies of the message.
BCC (Blind Carbon Copy)	Same as CC, except these names will not appear anywhere in the message, so other recipients will not know that the person(s) listed in the BCC field received a copy.
Group	Names of newsgroups that will receive this message (similar to Mail To).
Reply To	The e-mail address where replies should be sent.
Follow-up To	Another newsgroup heading; used to identify newsgroups to which comments should be posted (similar to Reply To).

■ Click in the Subject field (or press Tab to move the cursor there) and type the subject of the message.

■ Click in the blank composition area below the Subject field and type the body of your message. Word wrap occurs automatically, and you can cut and paste quotes from other messages or text from other programs. You can also check the spelling of your message by clicking on the Spelling button ![Spelling](spelling icon) on the Message Composition toolbar and responding to the dialog prompts that follow.

Send Messages

■ Once you have created a message, you have three choices:

- to send the message immediately
- to store the message in the Unsent Messages folder to be sent later (File, Send Later)
- to save the message in the Drafts folder to be finished and sent later (File, Save Draft)

To send a message immediately:

- Click the Send button ![Send](send icon) on the Message Composition toolbar.

The Message Composition Toolbar

■ The toolbar in the Message Composition window has several features that are specific only to this screen.

■ Notice that the main toolbar buttons contain a task name and illustration.

Message Composition Toolbar

		Immediately sends current message.
		Used when replying to a message, the Quote feature allows you to include text from the original message.
		Select an address from the addresses stored in your personal address book to insert into address fields.
		By clicking the Attach button, you can send a file, a Web page, or your personal address card along with your e-mail message.
		Checks for spelling errors in the current message.

Lets you save your message as a draft for later use.

 Sets the security status of a message.

 Stops the display of an HTML message or a message with an HTML attachment.

■ The Formatting toolbar provides commands for applying styles, fonts, font size, bulleted lists, and inserting objects.

Reply to Mail

■ To reply to a message, select or open the message to reply to and

click the Reply button [Reply].

■ From the submenu that appears, select Reply to Sender to reply to the original sender only, or select Reply to Sender and All Recipients to send a reply to the sender and all other recipients of the original message. Selecting one of these options lets you reply to the message without having to enter the recipient's name or e-mail address.

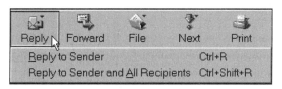

√ *The Message Composition window opens, with the To, Cc, and Subject fields filled in for you.*

■ Compose your reply as you would a new message.

■ To include a copy of the original message with your reply, click the

Quote button [Quote] on the Message Composition toolbar. You can edit the original message and header text as you wish.

■ When you are finished, click the Send button [Send] to send the message immediately.

Forward Mail

- To forward a message automatically without having to enter the recipient's name or e-mail address, first select or open the message to forward. Then click on the Forward button .

  The Message Composition window opens, with the Subject field filled in for you.

  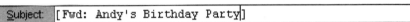

- Type the e-mail address of the new recipient in the To field, or click the Address button Address on the Message Composition toolbar and select a name from your Address Book (see "Address a New Message Using the Personal Address Book" on page 26 for information on using the Address Book).

- If the original message does not appear in the composition area, click the Quote button Quote on the Message Composition toolbar to insert it.

- Click in the composition area and edit the message as desired. You can also type any additional text you want to include with the forwarded message.

- When you are done, click the Send button Send to send the message immediately. Or, select Send Later from the File menu to store the message in the Unsent Messages mailbox to be sent later. To save the reply as a draft to be edited and sent later, select Save Draft from the File menu.

Add Entries to the Personal Address Book

- You can compile a personal address book to store e-mail addresses and other information about your most common e-mail recipients. You can then use the address book to find and automatically insert an address when creating a new message.

- To add a name to the address book:
  - Select Address Book from the Communicator menu. The Address Book window displays.

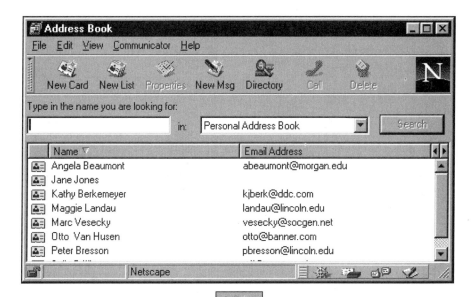

- Click the New Card button 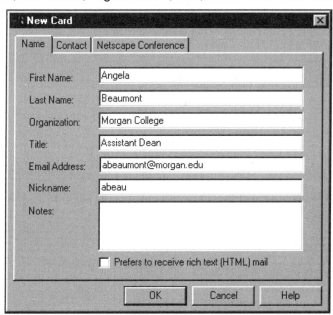 on the Address Book toolbar.
- In the New Card box that appears, enter the recipient's first name, last name, organization, title, and e-mail address.

- In the Nickname field, type a nickname for the recipient, if desired (the nickname must be unique among the entries in your address book). When addressing a message, you can use the recipient's nickname in the To field, rather than typing the entire address, and Messenger will automatically fill in the full e-mail address.

- In the Notes field, type any notes you want to store about the recipient.
- Click the Contact tab, if desired, and enter the recipient's postal address and phone number.
- Click OK.

■ You can edit an address book entry at any time by double-clicking on the person's name in the Address Book window.

■ You can automatically add the name and address of the sender of a message you are reading by selecting Add to Address Book from the Message menu and selecting Sender from the submenu. The New Card dialog box opens, with the First Name, Last Name, and E-mail Address fields filled in for you. You can enter a nickname for the person, if desired, and any other information you want in the remaining fields.

Address a New Message Using the Personal Address Book

■ To insert an address from your address book into a new message:

- Click the New Msg button [New Msg] to open the Message Composition window.

- Click on the Address button [Address] on the Message Composition toolbar and select a recipient(s) from the list in the Address Book window. Drag the selected name(s) into the To field in the Message Composition window. Click the Close button [X] in the Address Book window when you are finished.

  OR

- Begin typing the name or nickname of the recipient in the To field of the Message Composition window. If the name is included in the Address Book, Messenger will recognize it and finish entering the name and address for you.

Netscape Messenger: 6

◆ Attached Files ◆ View File Attachments
◆ Save Attached Files ◆ Attach Files to Messages

Attached Files

■ Sometimes an e-mail message will come with a separate file(s) attached. Messages containing attachments are indicated when you display a message and it contains a paperclip icon to the right of the message header. Attachment can be used, for example, when you want to send someone an Excel spreadsheet or a video clip.

■ With Messenger, you can view both plain text attachments and binary attachments. **Binary** files are files containing more than plain text (i.e., images, sound clips, and formatted text, such as spreadsheets and word processor documents).

■ Almost any e-mail program can read plain text files. Binary files, however, must be decoded by the receiving e-mail program before they can be displayed in readable form. This requires that the e-mail software have the capability to decode either MIME (Multi-Purpose Internet Mail Extension) or UUEncode protocol. Messenger can decode both. When a binary attachment arrives, Messenger automatically recognizes and decodes it.

View File Attachments

■ File or HTML attachments are displayed in one of two ways.

• If you select View, Attachments, Inline, you see the attachment appended to the body of the message in a separate attachment window below the message. Essentially there is a series of sequential windows—one with the message and the other with the attachment.

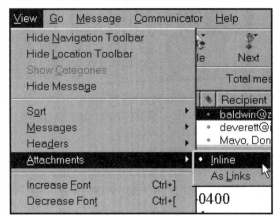

√ *Only plain text, images, and Web page attachments can be viewed inline.*

- If the attachment is HTML code, you will see a fully formatted Web page.

- If you select View, Attachments, As Links, the attachment window displays an attachment box displaying the details of the attachment. It also serves as a link to the attachment.

√ *Viewing attachments as links reduces the time it takes to open a message on screen.*

- Clicking on the blue-highlighted text in the attachment box will display the attachment.

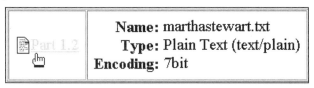

- You can right-click on the attachment icon box to display a menu of mail options such as forwarding, replying, or deleting the message.

  - By right-clicking on the actual attachment, you can choose from several file save options, such as saving the image or file in a separate file on your hard drive, as Windows wallpaper, or saving the image and putting a shortcut to the image on your desktop.

  - If you open a Web page attachment while online, you will find that the Web page serves as an actual connection to the Web site and that all links on the page are active. If you are not connected, the Web page will display fully formatted, but it will not be active.

- If an attached image displays as a link even after you select View, Attachments, Inline, it is probably because it is an image type that Messenger does not recognize. In this case, you need to install

28

and/or open a plug-in or program with which to view the unrecognized image.

- If you know you have the appropriate application or plug-in installed, click the Save File button in the Unknown File Type dialog box and save the attachment to your hard drive or disk (see "Save Attached Files" below). Then start the necessary application or plug-in and open the saved attachment file to view it.

- If you do not have the necessary application or plug-in, click on the More Info button in the Unknown File Type dialog box. The Netscape Plug-in Finder Web page opens, displaying some general information about plug-ins, a list of plug-ins that will open the selected attachment, and hyperlinks to Web sites where you can download the given plug-ins.

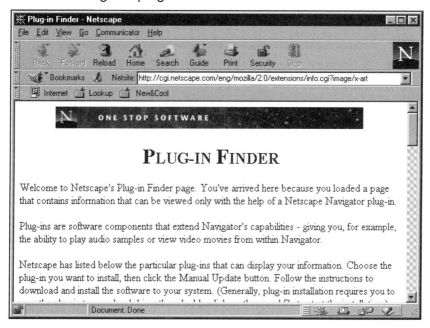

Save Attached Files

- You can save an attached file to your hard drive or disk for future use or reference. To save an attachment:

  - Open the message containing the attachment to save.

  - If the attachment is in inline view, convert it to a link (View, Attachments, As Links).

  - Right-click on the link and select Save Link As.

OR

- Click on the link to open the attachment. Select File, Save As, or, if Messenger does not recognize the attachment's file type, click the Save File button in the Unknown File Type dialog box.

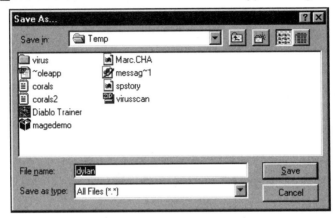

- In the Save As dialog box that follows, click the Save in drop-down list box and select the drive and folder(s) in which to save the file.
- Click in the File name text box and type a name for the file.
- Click Save.

Attach Files to Messages

- With Messenger, you can attach both plain text and binary files (images, media clips, formatted text documents, etc.) to e-mail messages. You may wish to check if your recipient's e-mail software can decode MIME or UUEncode protocols. Otherwise, binary attachments will not open and display properly on the recipient's computer.

- To attach a file to an e-mail message:

- Click the Attach button [Attach] on the Message Composition toolbar, and select File from the drop-down menu that appears.
- In the Enter file to attach dialog box that follows, click the Look in drop-down list box and select the drive and folder containing the file to attach.
- Then select the file to attach and click Open.

- After you have attached a file, the Attachments field in the Mail Composition window displays the name and location of the attached file.

  √ *Messages containing attachments usually take longer to send than those without attachments. When attaching very large files or multiple files, you may want to zip (compress) the files before attaching them. To do so, both you and the recipient need a file compression program, such as WinZip or PKZip.*

Attach Files and Documents

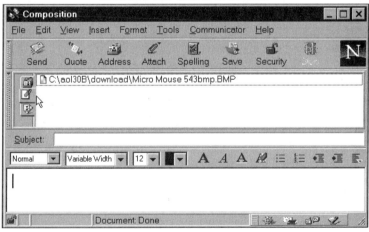

- Once you have attached the desired files and finished composing your message, you can send the e-mail, save it in the Unsent Messages folder for later delivery, or save it as a draft for later editing.

Microsoft Internet Explorer: 7

◆ **Start Internet Explorer 4**
◆ **Internet Explorer Screen** ◆ **Exit Internet Explorer**

Start Internet Explorer 4

■ When you first install Internet Explorer and you are using the Active Desktop, you may see the message illustrated below when you turn on your computer. If you are familiar with Explorer 3, you may want to select 1 Take a Quick Tour to learn the new features in Explorer 4. Select 2 to learn about Channels.

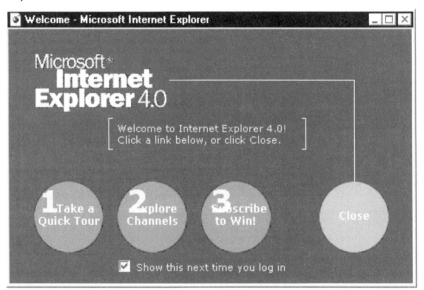

■ To start Internet Explorer, do one of the following:

• Click [Internet Explorer icon] on the Desktop.

OR

• Click [icon] on the taskbar.

OR

• Click the Start button [Start], then select Programs, Internet Explorer, and click Internet Explorer.

32

Internet Explorer Screen

- When you connect to the World Wide Web, the first screen that displays is called a home page. The term home page can be misleading since the first page of *any* World Wide Web site is called a home page. This first page is also sometimes referred to as the start page. You could think of the home/start page as the starting point of your trip on the information highway. Just as you can get on a highway using any number of on ramps, you can get on the Internet at different starting points.

- You can change the first page that you see when you connect to the Internet. To do this select View, Internet Options, then enter a new address in the Address text box.

  √ *The page that you see when you are connected may differ from the one illustrated below.*

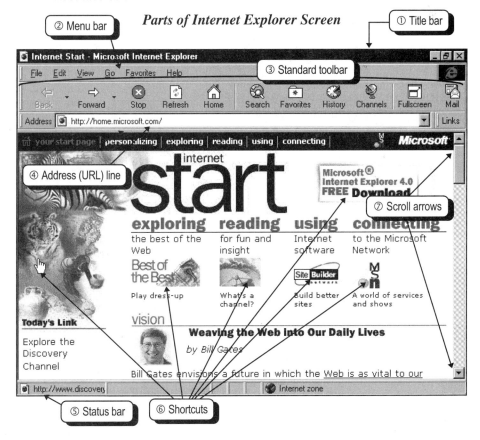

Parts of Internet Explorer Screen

② Menu bar ① Title bar ③ Standard toolbar ④ Address (URL) line ⑦ Scroll arrows ⑤ Status bar ⑥ Shortcuts

① **Title bar**   Displays the name of the program and the current Web page. You can minimize, restore, or close Explorer using the buttons on the right side of the Title bar.

② **Menu bar**   Displays menus currently available, which provide drop-down lists of commands for executing Internet Explorer tasks.

    The Internet Explorer icon on the right side of the Menu bar rotates when action is occurring or information is being processed.

③ **Standard toolbar**   Displays frequently used commands.

④ **Address (URL) line**   Displays the address of the current page. You can click here, type a new address, press Enter, and go to a new location (if it's an active Web site). You can also start a search from this line.

If you click on the arrow at the right end of the address line, you will see the links that you have visited during the current Internet session. The Links bar, containing links to various Microsoft sites is concealed on the right side of the address bar. Drag the split bar to the left or somewhere else on the screen to display current Links. If you double-click the Links button, all the current links will display. Double-click again to hide the links on the right side of the menu bar. You can add/delete links.

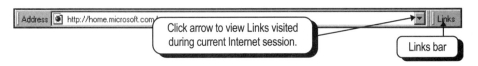

Links button

Buttons on Links bar

Note in the illustration above that the Links button has moved to the left side of the address bar. Just double-click on the Links button again to restore the address line. You can also drag the move bar, next to the Links button, to the left so that the Links and the Address line will both display. Drag the Links button down to display the contents of the Links bar directly below the Address bar (see illustration below).

⑤ **Status bar**   Displays information about actions occurring on the page and the Security Level. Internet Security Properties lets you control content that is downloaded on to your computer.

⑥ **Shortcuts**   Click on shortcuts (also called hyperlinks) to move to other Web sites. Shortcuts are usually easy to recognize. They can be underlined text, text of different colors, "buttons" of various sizes and shapes, or graphics. An easy way to tell if you are pointing to a shortcut is by watching the mouse pointer as it moves over the page. When it changes to a hand, you are on a shortcut. When you point to a shortcut the full name of the Web site will appear on the Status bar.

⑦ **Scroll arrows**   Scroll arrows are used to move the screen view, as in all Windows applications.

Exit Internet Explorer

■ Exiting Internet Explorer and disconnecting from your service provider are two separate steps. It is important to remember that if you close Internet Explorer (or any other browser), you must also disconnect (or hang up) from your service provider. If you don't disconnect, you'll continue incurring charges.

CAUTION	When you exit Internet Explorer, you do not necessarily exit from your Internet service provider. Be sure to check the disconnect procedure from your ISP so that you will not continue to be charged for time online. Some services automatically disconnect when a specific amount of time has passed with no activity.

Microsoft Internet Explorer: 8

◆ **Standard Toolbar Buttons**
◆ **Open a World Wide Web Site from the Address Bar**
◆ **Open a World Wide Web Site Using the File Open Dialog Box**

Internet Explorer Toolbar

Standard Toolbar Buttons

■ The **Internet Explorer Standard toolbar** displays frequently used commands. If the Standard toolbar is *not* visible when you start Explorer, open the View menu, select Toolbars, then select Standard Buttons.

 Moves back through pages previously displayed. Back is available only if you have moved around among Web pages in the current Navigator session; otherwise, it is dimmed.

 Moves forward through pages previously displayed. Forward is available only if you have used the Back button; otherwise, it is dimmed.

 Interrupts the opening of a page that is taking too long to display. Some pages are so filled with graphics, audio, or video clips that delays can be expected.

 Reloads the current page.

 Returns you to your home page. You can change your home page to open to any Web site or a blank page (View, Internet Options, General).

 Allows you to select from a number of search services with a variety of options.

 Displays the Web sites that you have stored using the features available on the Favorites menu. Click Favorites button again to close the Favorites.

Displays links to Web sites that you have visited in previous days and weeks. You can change the number of days that sites are stored in your History folder (View, Internet Options). Click the History button again to close the History window.

 Displays the list of current channels on the Explorer bar. Click again to close the Channels window.

 Conceals Menu, titles, Status bar, and address line to make available the maximum screen space possible for viewing a Web page. Click it again to restore Menu, titles, Status bar, and address line.

 Displays a drop-down menu with various Mail and News options. You will learn about Outlook Express e-mail options in Chapters 10-12.

Open a World Wide Web Site from the Address Bar

- Click in the Address bar and start typing the address of the Web site you want to open. If you have visited the site before, Internet Explorer will try to complete the address automatically. If it is the correct address, press Enter to go to it. If it is not the correct address, type over the suggested address that displayed on the line. To see other possible matches, click the down arrow. If you find the one you want, click on it.

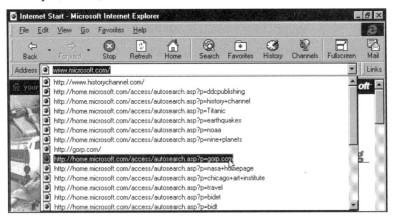

- To turn off the AutoComplete feature, open the View menu, select Internet Options, and click the Advanced tab. Deselect Use AutoComplete in the Browsing area of the dialog box.

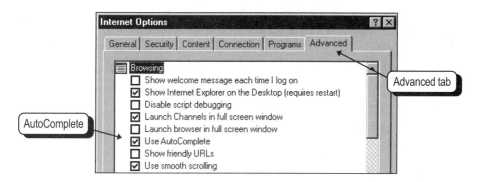

Open a World Wide Web Site Using the File Open Dialog Box

■ Select File, Open, and start entering the exact address of the site you want to open. If AutoComplete is turned on and Explorer finds a potential match for the site, it will automatically appear on this line. If the match is the site you want to open, press Enter to go there. If you want to see other possible matches, click the down arrow in the open dialog box.

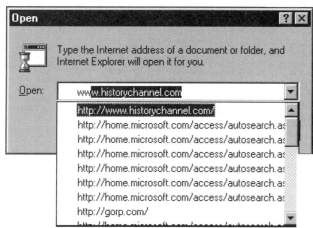

√ Other ways of opening Web sites will be explored in this lesson. Chapters 19-21 will explain how to search for sites whose exact addresses you do not know.

◆ **Open and Add to the Favorites Folder**
◆ **Open Web Sites from the Favorites Folder**
◆ **Create New Folders in the Favorites Folder**
◆ **AutoSearch from the Address Bar**

Open and Add to the Favorites Folder

- As you spend more time exploring Web sites, you will find sites that you want to visit frequently. You can store shortcuts to these sites in the **Favorites folder**.

- To add a site to the Favorites folder, first go to the desired Web site. Open the F<u>a</u>vorites menu or right-click anywhere on the page and select Add To <u>F</u>avorites.

- The following dialog box appears when you select Add to <u>F</u>avorites.

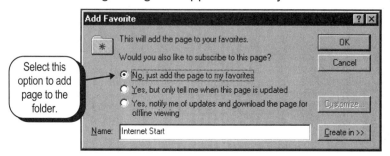

Select this option to add page to the folder.

- The name of the Page you have opened appears in the <u>N</u>ame box. There are three ways you can store the address in response to the question "Would you also like to subscribe to this page?" Subscribing to a page means you can schedule automatic updates to that site.

  - N<u>o</u>, just add the page to my favorites
    Puts a shortcut to the Web site in your Favorites folder.

  - <u>Y</u>es, but only tell me when this page is updated
    Explorer will alert you when an update to the site is available.

  - Yes, notify me of updates and <u>d</u>ownload the page for offline viewing
    Explorer will automatically download and update to your computer.

- Click OK to add the Web address to the Favorites folder.

Open Web Sites from the Favorites Folder

- Click the Favorites button Favorites on the Standard toolbar to open Web sites from the Favorites folder. The Explorer bar will open on the left side of the Browser window.

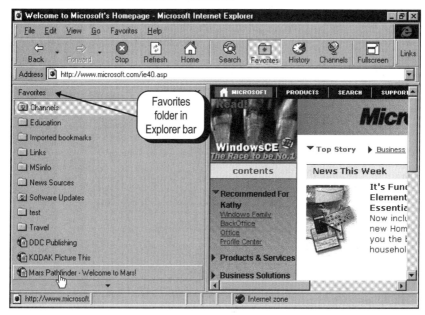

- Click on an address or open a folder and select a site. Close the Explorer bar by clicking the close button or the Favorites button on the toolbar.

- You can also open the Favorites menu and select a site from the list or from a folder.

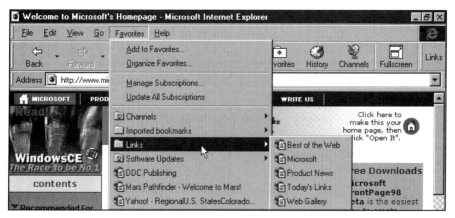

Create New Folders in the Favorites Folder

- You can create new folders before or after you have saved addresses in your Favorites folder.
  - Click Favorites and select Organize Favorites.
  - Click the Create New Folder button (shown in illustration below).

  - Type the name of the new folder and press Enter.

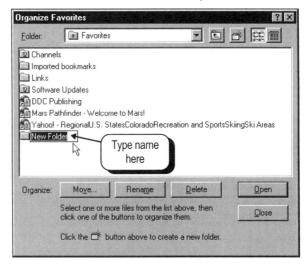

AutoSearch from the Address Bar

- In addition to displaying and entering addresses in the Address bar, you can use AutoSearch to perform a quick search directly from the Address bar.

- Click once in the Address bar and type *go*, *find*, or *?* and press the spacebar once. Enter the word or phrase you want to find and press Enter. For example, if you want to search for information about the year 2000, type "Find the year 2000" on the Address bar and press Enter.

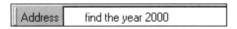

- Note the Status bar displays the message "Finding site…" It is actually finding a search site. In a few moments, the results of your search displays. The keywords in your search appear in bold in the list of links that are relevant to the search string that you entered.

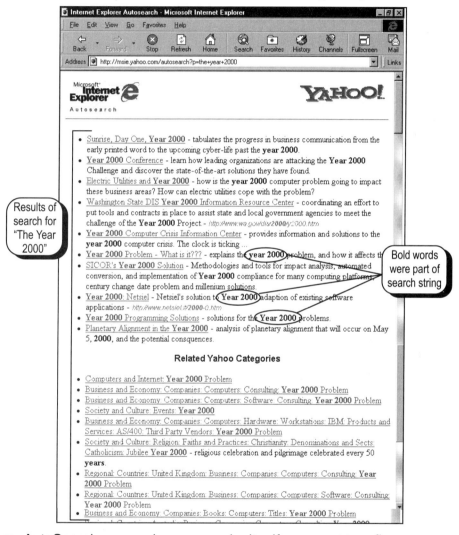

- AutoSearch uses only one search site. If you want to refine your search or see if other search engines will give you different results, click the Search button Search on the Standard toolbar and select a Search provider from the Choose provider drop-down list in the Explorer bar to access a different Search site.

Outlook Express: 10

◆ Configure Outlook Express ◆ Start Outlook Express
◆ Outlook Express Main Window ◆ Retrieve New Messages
◆ The Mail Window ◆ Read Messages ◆ Delete a Message
◆ Print a Message ◆ Save a Message

Configure Outlook Express

√ *This section assumes that you have already set up an e-mail account with a service provider. If you do not have an e-mail address, contact your Internet Service Provider. Establishing a modem connection and configuring your computer to send and receive mail can be frustrating. Don't be discouraged. What follows are steps that will get you connected, but some of the information may have to be supplied by your Internet Service Provider. Calling for help will save you time and frustration.*

■ Outlook Express is the e-mail program included in the Microsoft Internet Explorer 4.0 suite. With this program, you can send, receive, save, and print e-mail messages and attachments.

■ Before you can use Outlook Express to send and receive e-mail, you must configure the program with your e-mail account information (user name, e-mail address, and mail server names).

■ You may have already filled in this information if you completed the Internet Connection Wizard when you started Internet Explorer for the first time. If not, you can enter the information by running the Internet Connection Wizard again.

Internet Connection Wizard

• Launch Outlook Express. Open the Tools menu, select Accounts. Click the Mail tab. Click Add and select Mail to start the Connection Wizard.

• The Internet Connection Wizard will ask for information necessary to set up or add an e-mail account.

• Enter the name you want to appear on the "From" line in your outgoing messages. Click Next.

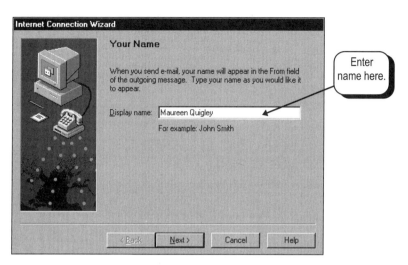

- Type your e-mail address. This is the address that people use to send mail to you. You usually get to create the first part of the address (the portion in front of the @ sign); the rest is assigned by your Internet Service Provider. Click Next.

- Enter the names of your incoming and outgoing mail servers. Check with your Internet Service Provider if you do not know what they are. Click Next.

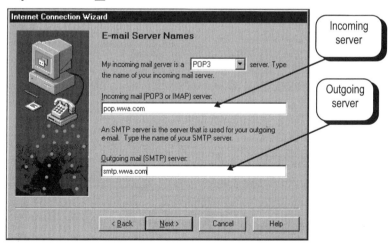

- Enter the logon name that your Internet Service Provider requires for you to access your mail. You will probably also have to enter a password. The password will appear as asterisks (******) to prevent others from knowing it. Click Next when you are finished.

- Enter the name of the account that will appear when you open the <u>A</u>ccounts list on the <u>T</u>ools menu in Outlook Express. It can be any name that you choose. Click <u>N</u>ext when you have finished.

- Select the type of connection that you are using to reach the Internet. If you are connecting through a phone line, you will need to have a dial-up connection. If you have an existing connection, click <u>N</u>ext and select from the list of current connections.

- Select an existing dial-up connection, or select <u>C</u>reate a new dial-up connection and follow the directions to create a new one.

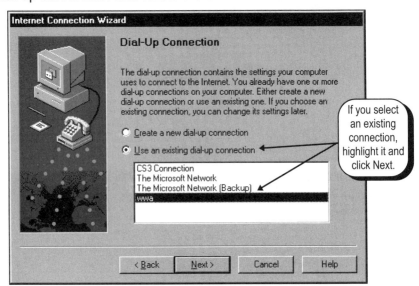

- If you select <u>U</u>se an existing dial-up connection you will click Finish in the last window to save the settings. You should then be able to launch Outlook Express and send and receive mail and attachments.

Start Outlook Express

- To start Outlook Express:

- Click the Mail icon ![mail icon] on the taskbar.

  √ *There is a chance that clicking the Mail icon from the Explorer main window will take you to the Microsoft Outlook organizational program. To use the more compact Outlook Express as your default mail program, click <u>V</u>iew, Internet <u>O</u>ptions from the Explorer main window. Click the Programs tab and choose Outlook Express from the <u>M</u>ail pull-down menu.*

  √ *If you downloaded Internet Explorer 4, be sure that you downloaded the standard version, which includes Outlook Express in addition to the Web browser.*

Outlook Express Main Window

■ After you launch Outlook Express, the main Outlook Express window opens by default. You can access any e-mail function from this window.

Outlook Express Main Window

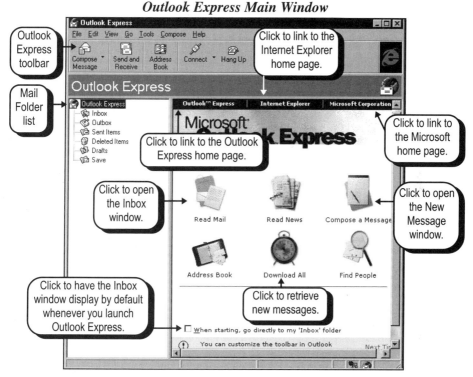

■ Descriptions of items in the main window follow below:

- The **Mail Folder list** displays in the left column of the window, with the Outlook Express main folder selected. To view the contents of a different folder, click on the desired folder in the folder list.

- **Shortcuts** to different e-mail functions are located in the center of the window. Click once on a shortcut to access the indicated task or feature.

- **Hyperlinks** to Microsoft home pages are located at the top of the window. Click once to connect to the indicated home page.

- The **Outlook Express toolbar** displays buttons for commonly used commands. Note that each button contains an image and text that describes the button function. Move your cursor over the button to display specific function information. Clicking any of these buttons will activate the indicated task immediately.

Retrieve New Messages

- You can access the retrieve new mail command from any Outlook Express window. To do so:

  - Click the Send and Receive button 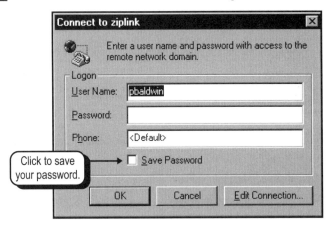 on the toolbar.

- In the Connection dialog box that displays, enter your ISP user name in the User Name text box and your password in the Password text box and click OK. (If you do not know your user name or password, contact your ISP.) Outlook Express will send this information to your ISP's mail server in order to make a connection.

  √ *Outlook Express will automatically save your user name and password for the rest of the current Internet session. However, you must re-enter your password each time you reconnect to the Internet or retrieve new mail, unless you set Outlook Express to save your password permanently. To do so, select the* **Save Password** *check box in the connection dialog box and click OK.*

- Once you are connected to the Internet and Outlook Express is connected to your ISP mail server, new mail messages will begin downloading from your ISP mail server. A dialog box displays the status of the transmittal.

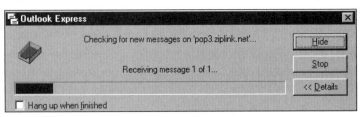

The Mail Window

- After retrieving new messages, Outlook Express stores them in the Inbox folder.

- To view your new messages, you must open the Mail window and display the contents of the Inbox folder. To do so:

  - Click the Read Mail shortcut | Read Mail | in the Outlook Express main window.

- The Mail window opens with the Inbox folder displayed. A description of the items in the Mail window appears on the following page:

Mail Window with Inbox Folder Displayed

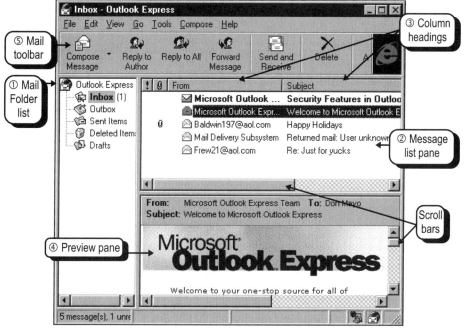

√   *In the message list, unread messages are displayed in bold text with a sealed envelope icon* ✉ *to the left of the header. Messages that have been read are listed in regular text with an open envelope icon* ✉ *to the left of the header.*

① The **Mail Folder list** displays the currently selected message folder, the contents of which are displayed in the mail list. Click on another folder to display its contents in the mail list.

② The **message list pane** displays a header for each of the messages contained in the currently selected mail folder.

③ **Column headings** list the categories of information included in each message header, such as subject, from, and date received. You can customize the display of the header columns in a number of ways:

- Resize column widths by placing the mouse pointer over the right border of a column heading until the pointer changes to a double arrow and then click and drag the border to the desired size.

- Rearrange the order of the columns by clicking and dragging a column heading to a new location in the series.

④ The **preview pane** displays the content of the message currently selected from the message list. You can show/hide the preview pane by selecting View, Layout and clicking on the Use preview pane check box. You can resize the preview pane or the message list pane by placing the pointer over the border between the two panes until the pointer changes to a double arrow and then dragging the border up or down to the desired size.

⑤ The **Mail toolbar** displays command buttons for working with messages. These commands vary depending on the message folder currently displayed (Inbox, Sent, Outbox, etc.).

Read Messages

√ *You do not have to be online to read e-mail. You can reduce your online charges if you disconnect from your ISP after retrieving your messages and read them offline.*

- You must have the Mail window open and the mail folder containing the message to read displayed.

- You can read a message in the preview pane of the Mail window, or in a separate window.

- To read a message in the preview pane, click on the desired message header in the message list. If the message does not appear, select View, Layout, Use preview pane.

- To open and read a message in a separate window, double-click on the desired message header in the message list.

  √ *The Message window opens displaying the Message toolbar and the contents of the selected message.*

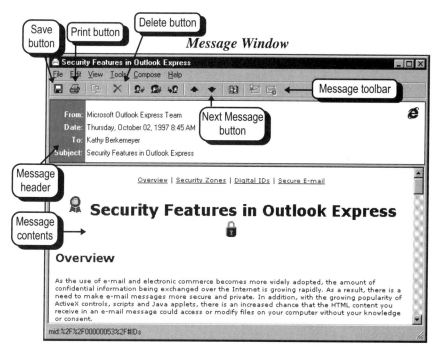

Message Window

- You can close the Message window after reading a message by clicking File, Close or by clicking on the Close button (X) in the upper-right corner of the window.

- Use the scroll bars in the Message window or the preview pane to view hidden parts of a displayed message. Or, press the down arrow key to scroll down through the message.

- To read the next unread message:

  - Select View, Next, Next Unread Message.

    OR

  - If you are viewing a message in the Message window, click the Next button [▼] on the Message toolbar.

- Once you have read a message, it remains stored in the Inbox folder until you delete it or file it in another folder. (See "Delete a Message" on the following page.)

Delete a Message

- To delete a message:
  - Select the desired header from the message list in the Mail window.
  - Click the Delete button ![X Delete] in the Mail toolbar, or select Edit, Delete.

  OR
  - Open the desired message in the Message window.
  - Click the Delete button ![X] on the Message toolbar.

  √ *To select more than one message to delete, click the Ctrl button while you click each message header.*

Print a Message

- To print a message:
  - Select the message you want to print from the message list in the Mail window or open the message in the Message window.
  - Select Print from the File menu.
  - In the Print dialog box that opens, select the desired print options and click OK.

Print Dialog Box

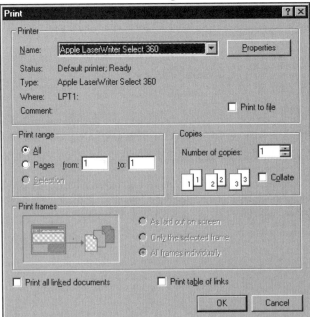

■ You can bypass the Print dialog box and send the message to the printer using the most recently used print settings by opening the message in the Message window and clicking the Print button 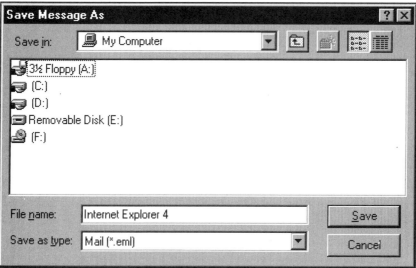 on the Message toolbar.

Save a Message

■ To save a message to your hard drive:

- Open the desired message in the Message window and click the Save button 🖫 on the Message toolbar.

- In the Save Message As dialog box that opens, click the Save in drop-down list box and select the drive and folder in which to store the message file.

Save Messages As

- Click in the File name box and enter a name for the message.
- Click Save.

Outlook Express: 11

◆ **Compose New Messages** ◆ **Send Messages** ◆ **Reply to Mail**
◆ **Forward Mail** ◆ **Add Entries to the Personal Address Book**
◆ **Address a New Message Using the Personal Address Book**

Compose New Messages

■ You can compose an e-mail message in Outlook Express while you are connected to the Internet, or while you are offline. When composing an e-mail message online, you can send the message immediately after creating it. When composing a message offline, you will need to store the message in your Outbox folder until you are online and can send it. (See "Send Messages" on page 56.)

■ To create a message, you first need to open the New Message window. To do so:

- Click the New Mail Message button on the toolbar in either the Mail window or the Main window.

  The New Message window displays (see the next page).

  √ *You can hide any toolbar in the New Message window by going to the View menu and deselecting Toolbar, Formatting Toolbar, or Status Bar.*

- In the New Message window, type the Internet address(es) of the message recipient(s) in the To field.

  √ *If you type the first few characters of a name or e-mail address that is saved in your address book, Outlook Express will automatically complete it for you. (See page 60 for information on using the Address Book.)*

  OR

  Click the Index Card icon in the To field or the Address Book button on the New Message toolbar and select an address to insert (see page 60 for information on using the Address Book).

  √ *If you are sending the message to multiple recipients, insert a comma or semicolon between each recipient's address.*

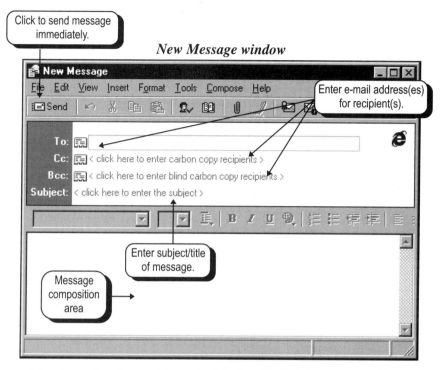

New Message window

- After inserting the address(es) in the To field, you may click in either of the following fields and enter the recipient information indicated.

| **CC (Carbon Copy)** | The e-mail addresses of people who will receive copies of the message. |
| **BCC (Blind Carbon Copy)** | Same as CC, except these names will not appear anywhere in the message, so other recipients will not know that the person(s) listed in the BCC field received a copy. |

- Click in the Subject field and type the subject of the message. An entry in this field is required.

- Click in the blank composition area below the Subject field and type the body of your message. Wordwrap occurs automatically, and you can cut and paste quotes from other messages or text from other programs. You can also check the spelling of your message by selecting Spelling from the Tools menu and responding to the prompts that follow.

Send Messages

- Once you have created a message, you have three choices:
  - to send the message immediately
  - to store the message in the Outbox folder to be sent later
  - to save the message in the Drafts folder to be edited and sent later

To send a message immediately:

√ *To be able to send messages immediately, you must first select Options from the Tools menu in the Mail window. Then click on the Send tab and select the Send messages immediately check box. If this option is not selected, clicking the Send button will not send a message immediately, but will send the message to your Outbox until you perform the Send and Receive task.*

- Click the send button 〔🖃 Send〕 on the New Message toolbar.

  OR

  Click File, Send Message.

- Outlook Express then connects to your ISP's mail server and sends out the new message. If the connection to the mail server is successful, the sending mail icon displays in the lower-right corner of the status bar until the transmittal is complete:

- Sometimes, however, Outlook Express cannot immediately connect to the mail server and instead has to store the new message in the Outbox for later delivery. When this happens, the sending mail icon does not appear, and the number next to your Outbox folder increases by one 〔⌐🍥 **Outbox** [1]〕.

- Outlook Express does not automatically reattempt to send a message after a failed connection. Instead, you need to manually send the message from the Outbox (see "To send messages from your Outbox folder" on page 57).

To store a message in your Outbox folder for later delivery:

- Select File, Send Later in the New Message window.

- The Send Mail prompt displays, telling you that the message will be stored in our Outbox folder.

- Click OK.

- The message is saved in the Outbox.

To send messages from your Outbox folder:

- Click on the Send and Receive button 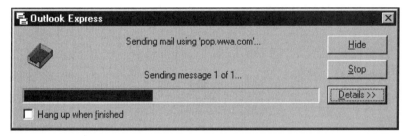 on the toolbar.

  OR

- Click Tools, Send and Receive, All Accounts.

√ *When you use the Send and Receive command, Outlook Express sends out **all** messages stored in the Outbox and automatically downloads any new mail messages from the mail server.*

- After you click Send and Receive, a dialog box opens, displaying the status of the transmittal.

To save a message to your Drafts folder:

- Click File, Save.
- The Saved Message prompt displays. Click OK.

To edit and send message drafts:

- In the Mail window, click in the Drafts folder Drafts (1) from the Mail Folder list.
- Double-click on the desired message header from the message list.
- In the New Message window that appears, edit your message as necessary. When you are finished, select File, Send Message to

send the message immediately, or Eile, Send Later to store it in the Outbox folder for later delivery.

■ Outlook Express automatically saves all sent messages in the Sent Items folder. To view a list of the messages you have sent, select the Sent Items folder ┊┈▢ Sent Items┊ from the Mail Folder list. The contents will display in the message list pane.

Reply to Mail

■ In Outlook Express, you can reply to a message automatically, without having to enter the recipient's name or e-mail address.

■ When replying, you have a choice of replying to the author and all recipients of the original message or to the author only.

■ To reply to the author and all recipients:

- Select the message you want to reply to from the message list in the Mail window.

- Click the Reply to All button ┊Reply to All┊ on the Mail toolbar.
  OR
- Right-click on the selected message and select Reply to All.

■ To reply to the author only:

- Click the Reply to Author button ┊Reply to Author┊ on the Mail toolbar.
  OR
- Right-click on the selected message and select Reply to Author.

■ Once you have selected a reply command, the New Message window opens with the address fields and the Subject filled in for you.

√ *You can access all of the mail send commands by right-clicking on the message in the Message list.*

58

- The original message is automatically included in the body of your response. To turn off this default insertion, select Options from the Tools menu, click on the Send tab, deselect the Include message in reply check box, and click OK.

- To compose your reply, click in the composition area and type your text as you would in a new message.

- When you are done, click the Send button [Send] on the New Message toolbar to send the message immediately. Or, select Send Later from the File menu to store the message in the Outbox folder for later delivery. To save the reply as a draft to be edited and sent later, select Save from the File menu.

Forward Mail

- To forward a message automatically without having to enter the message subject:

  - Select the message to forward from the message list in the Mail window.

  - Click the Forward Message button [Forward Message] on the Mail toolbar.

    The New Message window opens with the original message displayed and the Subject field filled in for you.

- Fill in the e-mail address information by either typing each address or selecting the recipients from your address book. (See "Address a New Message Using the Personal Address Book" on page 62.)

  √ *If you are forwarding the message to multiple recipients, insert a comma or semicolon between each recipient's address.*

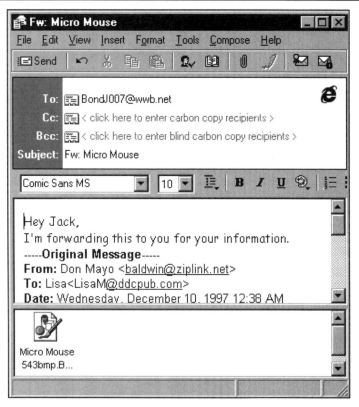

- Click in the composition area and type any text you wish to send with the forwarded message.

- When you are done, click the Send button ⌐Send on the New Message toolbar to send the message immediately. Or, select Send Later from the File menu to store the message in the Outbox folder for later delivery. To save the reply as a draft to be edited and sent later, select Save from the File menu.

Add Entries to the Personal Address Book

- In Outlook Express, you can use the Windows Address Book to store e-mail addresses and other information about your most common e-mail recipients. You can then use the Address Book to find and automatically insert addresses when creating new messages.

- To open the Windows Address Book:

  - Click the Address Book button 📖 on the toolbar in the Mail window or the Main window.

The Address Book window opens, displaying a list of contacts.

Address Book Window

Address Book - [C:\WINDOWS\Application Data\Microsoft\Address Book\K...

File   Edit   View   Tools   Help

New Contact   New Group   Properties   Delete   Find   Print   Send Mail

Type name or select from list:

Name ▲	E-Mail Address	Business Phone	Home Phone
Abercromby, Laura	abercromby@gate.com		
Abrams, Sally	sabrams@banner.com		
Achner, Michael	mikeachner@banner.com		
Alan, Edward	edalan@gate.com		
Albany, Richard	ralban@depot.net		
Alders, Josephine	joalders@morgan.edu		
Allison, Leslie	lallison@morgan.edu		
Anderson, Beatrice	beatrice@depot.net		

81 items

■ To add a name to the address book:

• Click the New Contact button |New Contact| on the Address Book toolbar.

• In the Properties dialog box that displays, type the First, Middle and Last names of the new contact in the appropriate text boxes.

• Type the contact's e-mail address in the Add new text box and then click the Add button. You can repeat this procedure if you wish to list additional e-mail addresses for the contact.

• In the Nickname text box, you can enter a nickname for the contact (the nickname must be unique among the entries in your address book). When addressing a new message, you can type the nickname in the To field, rather than typing the entire address, and Outlook Express will automatically complete the address.

Contact Properties Dialog Box

Properties

Personal | Home | Business | Other | Conferencing | Digital IDs

Enter personal information about this contact here.

Name
First: Middle: Last:
Display: Nickname:

E-Mail Addresses
Add new: Add

Edit
Remove
Set as Default

☐ Send E-Mail using plain text only.

OK   Cancel

- You can automatically add the name and address of the sender of a message by opening the message in the Message window, right-clicking on the sender's name in the To field, and selecting Add to Address Book from the shortcut menu.

- You can also set Outlook Express to add the address of recipients automatically when you reply to a message. To do so, select Options from the Tools menu and select the Automatically put people I reply to in my Address Book check box on the General tab.

- You can edit an Address Book entry at any time by double-clicking on the person's name in the contact list in the Address Book window.

Address a New Message Using the Personal Address Book

- To insert an address from your address book into a new message:

  - Click the Select Recipients button 📖 on the New Message toolbar.

  - In the Select Recipients dialog box that follows, select the address to insert from the contact list.

Select Recipients Dialog Box

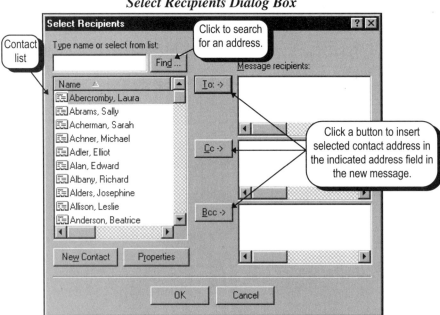

  - Click the button for the field in which you want to insert the address (To, Cc, or Bcc). Click OK to return to the New Message window when you are finished.

Outlook Express: 12

◆ **View Attached Files** ◆ **Save Attached Files** ◆ **Attach Files to a Message**

View Attached Files

■ Sometimes an e-mail message will come with a separate file(s) attached. Messages containing attachments are indicated in the message list in the Mail window by a paperclip icon 📎 to the left of the message header.

■ If the selected message is displayed in the preview pane, a larger paper clip attachment icon will appear to the right of the header at the top of the preview pane.

Mail Window

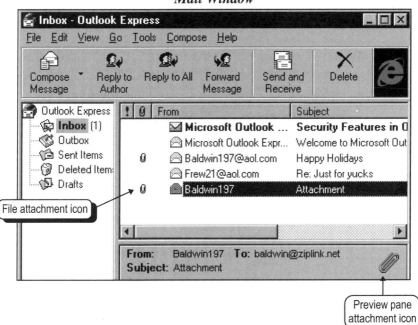

■ If you open the selected message in its own window, an attachment icon will appear in a separate pane below the message.

- To view an attachment:
  - Open the folder containing the desired message in the Mail window.
  - Select the message containing the desired attachment(s) from the message list to display it in the preview pane.

    If the attachment is an image, it will display in the message.

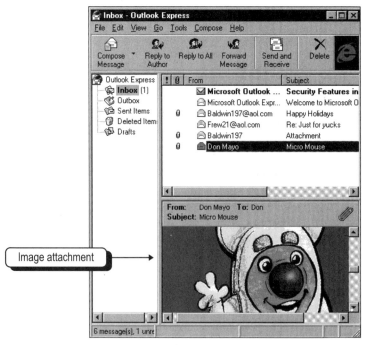

64

√ *If the image does not display, click Tools, Options, click the Read tab, select the Automatically show picture attachments in messages check box, and click OK.*

■ Other types of attachments, such as a program, word processor document, or media clip, do not display in the message, but have to be opened in a separate window. To do so:

• Click on the attachment icon 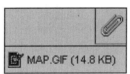 in the preview pane. A button will display with the file name and size of the attachment.

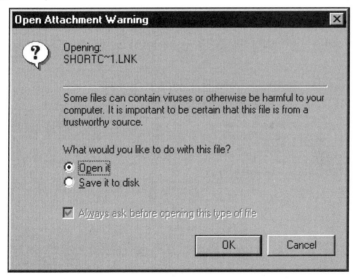

• Click on this button.

• If the Open Attachment Warning dialog box displays, select the Open it option and click OK.

■ Outlook Express will open the attached file or play the attached media clip.

■ If the attached file does not open, Outlook Express does not recognize the file type of the attached file (that is, Outlook Express does not contain the plug-in, or your computer does not contain the application needed to view it).

■ To view an unrecognized attachment, you have to install and/or open the application or plug-in needed to view it.

Save Attached Files

■ If desired, you can save an attached file to your hard drive or disk for future use or reference. To save an attachment:

- Select Save Attachments from the File menu, and select the attachment to save from the submenu that displays.

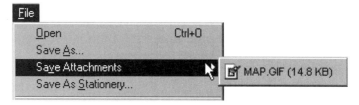

OR

- Right-click on the attachment icon 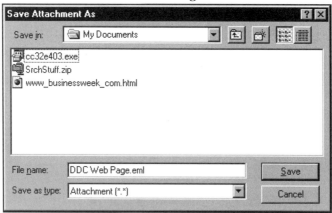 in the Message window and select the Save As option.

- In the Save As dialog box that follows, click the Save in drop-down list box and select the drive and folder in which to save the file.

Save As Dialog Box

- Click in the File name text box and type a name for the file.
- Click Save.

Attach Files to a Message

- You can attach a file to an e-mail message while composing the message in the New Message window. To add an attachment:

  - Click the Attachments button 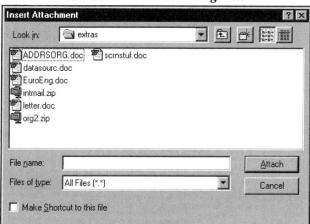 on the New Message toolbar.

  OR

  - Click Insert, File Attachment.

  - In the Insert Attachment dialog box that appears, click the Look in drop-down list box and select the drive and folder containing the file to attach. Then select the file and click Attach.

Insert Attachment Dialog Box

√ *The attachment will appear as an icon in the body of the message.*

√ *Messages containing attachments usually take longer to send than those without attachments.*

√ *When attaching very large files or multiple files, you may want to zip (compress) the files before attaching them. To do so, both you and the recipient need a file compression program, such as WinZip or PKZip.*

New Message Dialog Box

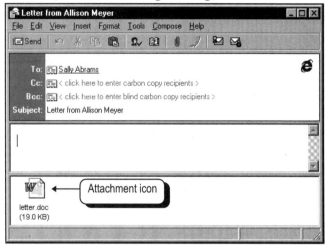

- You can also attach a file by dragging the desired file from your desktop or from Windows Explorer into the New Message window.

- You can add multiple attachments by repeating the procedure as many times as you like.

- Before you send a message containing an attachment, you may wish to make sure the recipient's e-mail program can decode the file you are sending.

America Online: 13

◆ **About America Online** ◆ **Start America Online**
◆ **The AOL Home Page, Menu, and Toobar** ◆ **AOL Help** ◆ **Exit AOL**

About America Online?

- America Online (AOL) is an all-purpose online service. Unlike Netscape Navigator or Microsoft Internet Explorer, AOL is not an Internet browser, yet you can browse the Internet using AOL navigation features.

- Unlike Internet browsers, AOL does not require a separate Internet Service provider for Internet access, nor does it require a separate mail server connection to access e-mail from the AOL Mail Center. When you install AOL, you configure the program to establish a dial-up connection to the AOL server using your modem. All connections to the Internet and the Mail Center are made via the AOL server.

  √ *An Internet service provider is a company that provides Internet access.*

Start America Online

- To start America Online (Windows 95):

  - Click the AOL icon on your desktop. This icon should display on your desktop after you install AOL.

    OR

    Click the Start button , Programs, America Online, America Online for Windows 95.

  - Make sure your screen name is displayed in the Select Screen Name box and type in your password in the Enter Password box.

  - Click the Sign On button to connect to the AOL server.

The AOL Home Page, Menu, and Toolbar

- After you successfully log on to America Online, you will see a series of screens. The final first screen you see is the AOL home page or start page. The AOL home page contains links to daily AOL featured areas as well as links to constant AOL areas such as **Channels** and **What's New**. You can also access your mailbox from the home page.

Home Screen Menu

- The AOL menu displays options currently available. Click the heading to display a drop-down menu of links to AOL areas and basic filing, editing, and display options.

America Online Toolbar

- The AOL toolbar contains buttons for AOL's most commonly used commands. Choosing a button activates the indicated task immediately.

	You have new mail if the flag on the mailbox is in the up position. Click to display a list of new mail in your mailbox.
	Compose and Send Mail Messages. Displays the Composition screen for composing new mail messages.

	Channels are areas of interest arranged by category. AOLs 21 channels offer hundreds of AOL areas and Web site connections.
	New and exciting AOL areas to explore including new AOL features, areas, and special interest sites.
	People Connection takes you to the AOL chat area. Here you can access the AOL Community Center, Chat Rooms, and meet the stars in the Live chat forum.
	File Search opens the search window to the software library where you can download hundreds of software programs.
	Stocks and Portfolios links you to the latest stock market quotes, research a company or mutual fund, or find the latest financial news.
	This area not only brings you the latest headline news, weather, and sports but also allows you to search news archives by keywords. You can also see multimedia (slide show and audio) presentations of the hottest topics in the news.
	Connects you to the Web.
	Shop Online in the AOL Marketplace. Goods and services are categorized for your convenience.
	Lets you customize AOL to suit your needs. Each member area shows you step-by-step how to access and select options.
	Click to see an estimate of how long you have been online for the current session.
	Click to print whatever is displayed on your computer screen. Opens the Print dialog box where you can select from the standard print options.
	The Personal Filing Cabinet is a storage area located on your hard disk used to organize files such as downloaded e-mail messages, files, and newsgroup messages.
	Click this icon to create links or shortcuts to your favorite Web sites or AOL areas.
	This is a quick way to access the AOL member directory and to find answers to questions.
	Displays an area called Find Central. Go here to search the AOL directory using keywords and phrases.
	Each AOL area has a keyword to identify the area. Enter the Keyword for immediate access to the desired AOL area.

AOL Help

- AOL offers extensive Help so that you can learn to use AOL effectively and find answers to any questions you may have about either AOL or the Web. All AOL topics can be printed or saved to your hard disk.

- To access Help, click Help and the help topic of choice from the menu.

Exit AOL

- To exit AOL, click the close window button ⊠ in the upper-right corner of the AOL screen.

  OR

  Click Sign Off, Sign Off on the menu bar.

  OR

  Click File, Exit.

America Online: 14

◆ **Access the Internet from AOL** ◆ **Open a Wold Wide Web Site**
◆ **The AOL Browser Screen** ◆ **Stop a Load or Search**

Access the Internet from AOL

■ To go to the Internet Connection:

- Click the Internet button [Internet] on the AOL main screen.

   OR

- Click [**internet**] from the Channels menu.

   OR

- Press Ctrl+K, type internet in the Keyword box and press Enter.
  The Internet Connection window displays.

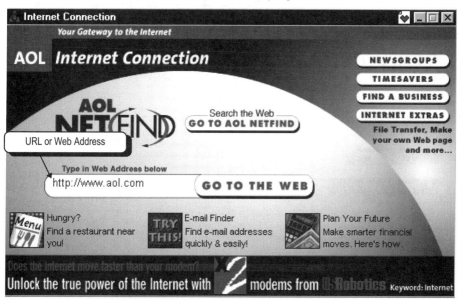

America Online (AOL) 73

Open a World Wide Web Site

- If you know the Web address (URL), type it into the Type in Web Address below box and click the GO TO THE WEB button
  [GO TO THE WEB] or press Enter. If the Web address is correct, you will be connected to the Web site.

- If you wish to search the Internet, click the GO TO AOL NETFIND button [GO TO AOL NETFIND].

The AOL Browser Screen

- Once you are connected to the Web, the screen elements change, and the Browser toolbar displays.

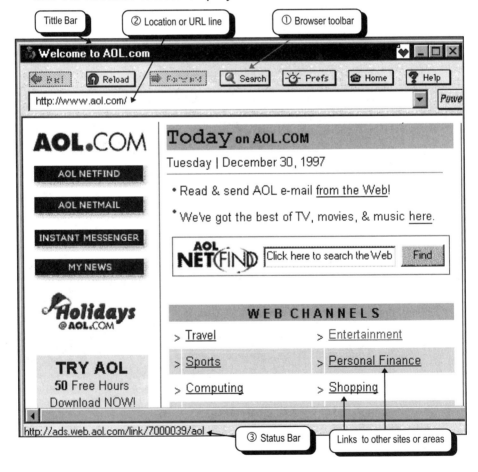

① **Browser Toolbar**

- The AOL Browser toolbar will help you navigate through sites you visit on the Web. Buttons on the Browser toolbar also connect you to search and Internet preference areas.

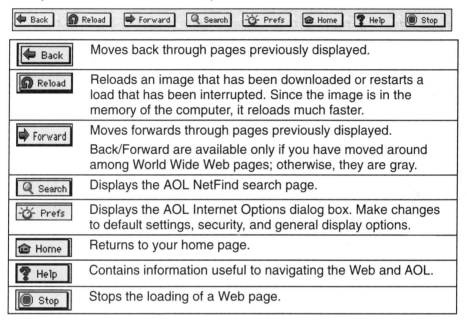

Back	Moves back through pages previously displayed.
Reload	Reloads an image that has been downloaded or restarts a load that has been interrupted. Since the image is in the memory of the computer, it reloads much faster.
Forward	Moves forwards through pages previously displayed. Back/Forward are available only if you have moved around among World Wide Web pages; otherwise, they are gray.
Search	Displays the AOL NetFind search page.
Prefs	Displays the AOL Internet Options dialog box. Make changes to default settings, security, and general display options.
Home	Returns to your home page.
Help	Contains information useful to navigating the Web and AOL.
Stop	Stops the loading of a Web page.

② **Location Line**

- AOL stores each Web address you visit during each AOL session. If you wish to return to an address you have visited during the current session, you can click the location box arrow and click the address from the pull-down list.

③ Status Bar

Status Message

- The Status bar, located at the bottom of the screen, is a helpful indicator of the progress of the loading of a Web page. For example, if you are loading a Web site, you will see the byte size of the page, the percentage of the task completed, and the number of graphics and links yet to load. In many cases the time it will take to load the page will display.

Stop a Load or Search

- Searching for information or loading a Web page can be time-consuming, especially if the Web page has many graphic images, if a large number of people are trying to access the site at the same time, or if your modem and computer operate at slower speeds. If data is taking a long time to load, you may wish to stop a search or the loading of a page or large file.

- To stop a search or load:

  - Click the Stop button ⬛ Stop on the Navigation toolbar.

- If you decide to continue the load after clicking the Stop button, click the Reload button 🔂 Reload.

America Online: 15

Favorite Places

- A **Favorite Place** listing is a bookmark that you create containing the title, URL, and a direct link to a Web page or AOL area that you may want to revisit. A Favorite Place listings links directly to the desired page.

- The AOL Favorite Place feature allows you to maintain a record of Web sites in your Favorite Places file so that you can return to them easily. (See "Add Favorite Places" below.)

Add Favorite Places

- There are several ways to mark an AOL area or Web site and save it as a Favorite Place. Once the page is displayed:

  - Click the Favorite Place heart 💟 on the Web site or AOL area title bar.

  TUCOWS World Wide Affiliate Site Locations! 💟 _ □ ✕

  - Click Yes to confirm the addition of the listing.

    > Favorite Place icon

  OR

  - Display the Web page to add, right-click anywhere on the page and select Add to Favorites from the shortcut menu.

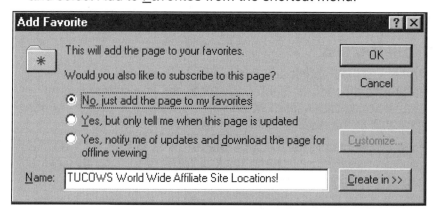

America Online (AOL) 77

- Click the desired option from the confirmation box that displays and click OK.
- The site will automatically be added to your Favorite Places list.

View Favorite Places

■ You can view the Favorite Places file by selecting Go To, Favorite

Places, or by clicking on the Favorite Places button on the AOL toolbar. Click on any listing from the list to go directly to that page.

■ The details of any Favorite Place listing can be viewed or modified by using the buttons on the Favorite Places screen.

Delete Favorite Places

■ You may wish to delete a Favorite Place if a Web site no longer exists or remove an AOL area from the listing that is no longer of interest to you.

To delete a Favorite Place:

- Click the Favorite Places button on the toolbar.
- Click on the listing to delete.
- Click the Delete button **Delete** from the Favorite Places screen.
  OR
- Right-click on the listing and select Delete from the pop-up menu.
  OR
- Press the Delete key.
- Click YES to confirm the deletion.

AOL History List

■ While you move back and forth within a Web site, AOL automatically records each page location. The history is only temporary and is deleted when you sign-off. AOL areas are not recorded in the history list.

■ To view the history list, click on the arrow at the end of the URL line. You can use History to jump back or forward to recently viewed pages by clicking on the page from the list.

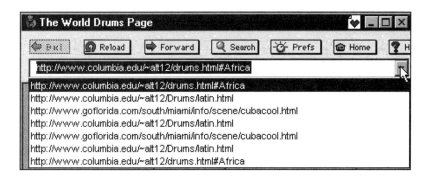

Save Web Pages

■ When you find a Web page with information that you would like to
keep for future reference, or to review later offline, you can save it
to your hard disk. To save a Web page:

- Click File, Save

- Type a filename in the File name box.

  √ *When you save a Web page, often the current page name appears in the*
  File name box. You can use this name or type a new one.

- Choose the drive and folder in which to store the file from the
  Save in drop-down list

- Click Save.

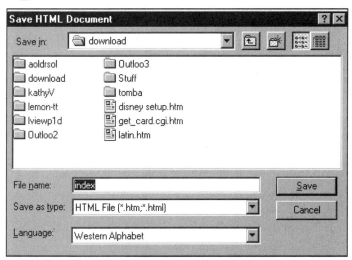

■ In most cases when you choose to save a Web page, AOL will
automatically save it as an HTML file. Saving a page as an HTML

file saves the original formatting and, when accessed, will display as you saw it on the Web.

- You can also save a Web page as a Plain text file which saves only the page text without the formatting or images and placeholders. You might want to do this when saving a very large file, such as a literary work or multiple-page article. To save in Plain text format, click the down arrow next to the Save as type box in the Save As dialog box and select Plain text from the list.

- You can view a saved Web page later by clicking File, Open, and entering the name and location from the Open a File box or by choosing the location and double-clicking on the file name.

Print Web Pages

- One of the many uses of the Internet is to find and print information. You can print a page as it appears on screen, or you can print it as plain text. Only displayed pages can be printed. To print a Web page, display it and do the following:

  - Click the Print button on the AOL toolbar.

  OR

  - Click Print on the File menu.

  - In the Print dialog box that displays, select the desired print options and click OK.

- In most cases, the Web page will be printed in the format shown in the Web page display.

America Online E-mail: 16

◆ Read New Mail ◆ Compose a New Mail Message
◆ Send Messages ◆ Reply to Mail
◆ Forward Mail ◆ AOL Mail Help

Read New Mail

■ There are several ways to know whether you have new mail in your mailbox: If your computer has a sound card and speakers, you will hear "You've Got Mail" when you successfully connect to AOL. The link is replaced by the You Have Mail link, and the mailbox

icon on the main screen has the flag in the up position .

To display and read new and unread mail:

- Click the You Have Mail button on the AOL main screen.
  OR
- Click the Read New Mail button on the main screen toolbar
  OR
- Press Ctrl+R.

  √   *The New Mail list displays new and unread mail for the screen name used for this session. If you have more than one screen name, you must sign on under each name to retrieve new mail.*

  √   *New and Unread e-mail messages remain on the AOL mail server for approximately 27 days before being deleted by AOL. If you want to save a message to your hard disk, click **File, Save As** and choose a location for the message. By default the message will be saved to the Download folder.*

- To read a message, double-click on it from the New Mail list.

Compose a New Mail Message

- Click <u>M</u>ail, <u>C</u>ompose Mail.
  OR
- Click the Compose Mail button on the main screen toolbar.
  OR
- Click Ctrl+M.

The Compose Mail screen displays.

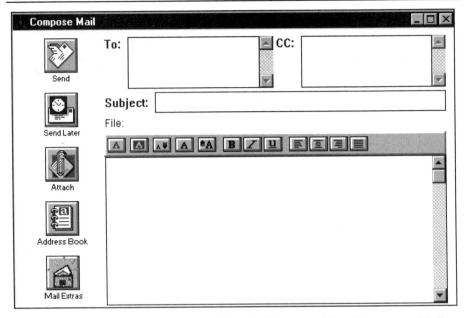

- Fill in the e-mail address(es) in the To box of the Compose Mail screen.

  OR

- Select Address Book and double-click to select an address. (See "America Online E-mail: 18" on page 88 for more information on your Address book.)

- If you are sending the same message to multiple recipients, fill in the CC: (Carbon Copy) box with the e-mail addresses of recipients who will receive a copy of this message. These names will display to all recipients of the message.

- If you want to send BCC: (Blind courtesy copies—copies of a message sent to others but whose names are not visible to the main or other recipients), put the address in parenthesis, for example: (ddcpub.com).

  √ *Multiple addresses must be separated with a comma.*

- Fill in the Subject box with a one-line summary of your message. AOL will not deliver a message without a subject heading. This is the first thing the recipient sees in the list of new mail when your message is delivered.

- Fill in the body of the message.

Send Messages

- Click the Send button [Send] to send the message immediately. *You must be online.*

  OR

- Click the Send Later button [Send Later] to send a message later that you have composed offline.

Reply to Mail

- You can reply to mail messages while online or compose replies to e-mail offline to send later.

- To reply to e-mail:

  - Click the Reply button [Reply] from the displayed message screen. If the message has been sent to more than one person, you can send your response to each recipient of the message by clicking the Reply to All button [Reply to All]. The addresses of the sender and, if desired, all recipients will be automatically inserted into the address fields.

    √ *To include part or all of the original message in your Reply, select the contents of the original message to be included in quotes in your message and click the Reply button to begin your reply.*

  - Click the Send button [Send] if you are online and want to send the reply immediately or click the Send Later button [Send Later].

Forward Mail

- There are times when you may want to send mail sent to you on to someone else.

- To forward e-mail:

  - Click the Forward button ⌷Forward⌷ from the displayed message screen and fill in the address(es) of the recipients of the forwarded message. The Subject heading from the original message is automatically inserted into the subject heading box.

  - Click the Send button ⌷ Send ⌷ if you are online and want to send

    the reply immediately or click the Send Later button ⌷Send Later⌷.

AOL Mail Help

- For answers to many of your basic e-mail questions, click Mail, Mail

  Center, and click on the Let's Get Started button 📷.

♦ **Add Attachments to a Message**
♦ **Download File Attachments**

Add Attachments to a Message

■ You can attach a file to send along with any e-mail message. Before you send a file attachment—especially if it is a multimedia file—it is a good idea to make sure that the recipient's e-mail program can read the attachment. For example, files sent in MIME format cannot be viewed by AOL e-mail and require separate software to be opened.

To attach files to a message:

• Compose the message to be sent. (See "Compose a New Mail Message" on page 81.)

• Click the Attach button [Attach] on the Compose Message screen.

• Select the drive and folder where the file you wish to attach is located.

• Double-click the file to attach from the Attach File dialog box.
  √ *The attachment will appear below the Subject box.*

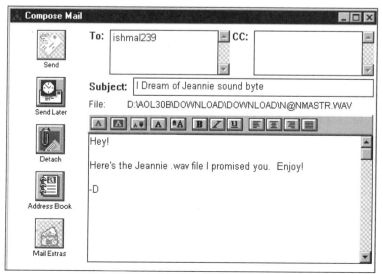

- If you are online, click the Send button [Send] to send the

  message immediately, or click the Send Later button [Send Later] to store the message in your Outgoing Mail if you are working offline.

  √ *Multiple files must be grouped together in a single archive using a file compression program such as PKZIP or WINZIP. Both you and the recipient will need a file compression program.*

Download E-mail File Attachments

- An e-mail message that arrives with a file attachment is displayed in your new mail list with a small diskette under the message icon.

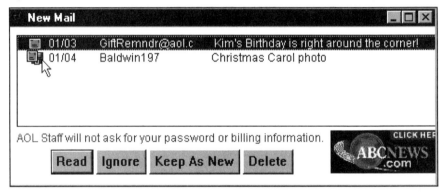

- Opening the message and viewing the attachment are two separate steps:

  - Open the message by double-clicking on it from the New Mail list (see "To display and read new and unread mail" on page 81). The message will display.

  - You can choose to download the file attachment immediately by clicking the Download File button [Download File] at the bottom of the displayed message screen. Click the Save button [Save] on the Download Manager screen to save the file, by default, to the AOL30/Download folder. If you desire, you can change the save destination folder.

- A status box will display while the attachment is being downloaded or transferred to your computer.

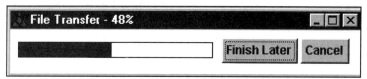

- At the end of the download, the file transfer box will close and you will see the message "File's Done."

OR

- You may choose to download the file later. Click the Download Later button **Download Later** to store the message in the Download Manager. When you are ready to download the file, click File, Download Manager, and then select the file to download. You must be online.

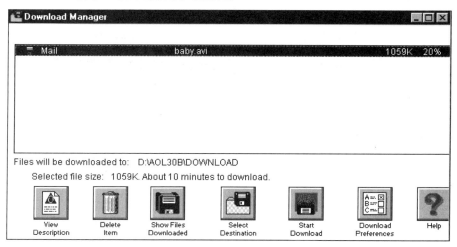

√ *Click Sign off after transfer if you want AOL to automatically disconnect when the transfer is complete.*

To change the default location of where files are stored:

- Click the Select Destination button from the Download Manager screen and choose the desired destination from the Select Path dialog box.

◆ **Add Entries to the Address Book**
◆ **Enter an Address Using the Address Book**

Add Entries to the Address Book

■ Once you start sending e-mail, you may be surprised at how many people you start to communicate with online. An easy way to keep track of e-mail addresses is to enter them into the Address Book. Once an e-mail address entry has been created, you can automatically insert it from the Address Book into the address fields.

To create Address Book entries:

- Click <u>M</u>ail, Edit <u>A</u>ddress Book. The Address Book dialog box displays.

- Click the Create button [**Create**] to open the Address Group box.

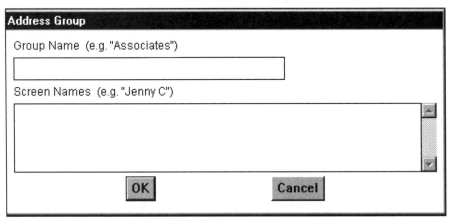

- Enter the real name or nickname of the e-mail recipient (e.g., JohnV) or the name of a Group listing (e.g., Book Club) in the Group Name box. The name you enter in this box is the name that will appear in the Address Book list.

- Press the Tab key to move to the Screen Names box and enter the complete e-mail address of the recipient or the e-mail addresses of everyone in the group listing. When entering multiple addresses such as in a group listing, each address must be separated by a comma (e.g., Baldwin168, BubbaB@ziplink.net, etc.).

- Click OK.

  √ *When sending mail to AOL members through AOL, you do not need to enter the @aol.com domain information. Enter only their screen name as the e-mail address. For all other Address Book entries you must enter the entire address.*

Delete an Address Book Entry

- Click <u>M</u>ail, Edit <u>A</u>ddress Book to open the Address Book.
- Click the name to delete.
- Click the Delete button Delete .
- Click Yes.
- Click OK to close the Address Book.

Enter an Address Using the Address Book

- Place the cursor in the desired address field.

- Click the Address Book button Address Book to open the Address Book.
- Double-click the name or names from the Address Book list to insert in the TO: or CC: address box and click OK.

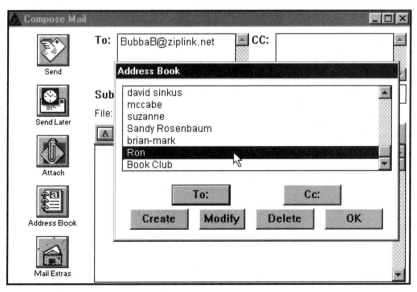

◆ **Searching vs. Surfing** ◆ **Search Sites** ◆ **Search Basics**

Searching vs. Surfing

- The Web is a vast source of information, but to find information that you want, you must be able to locate it. The Web has many thousands of locations, containing hundreds of thousands of pages of information.

- Unlike libraries that use either the Library of Congress or Dewey Decimal system to catalog information, the Internet has no uniform way of tracking and indexing information. You can find lots of information on the Internet; the trick is to find information that you want. Initially, it may seem easy to find information on the Web— you just connect to a relevant site and then start clicking on links to related sites. Illustrated below is an example of a search that starts out on one topic and ends on an unrelated one.

Both the Pathfinder lander and rover have stereo imaging systems. The rover, additionally, carries an alpha proton x-ray spectrometer with which it will examine the composition of the rocks. The imaging system will reveal the mineralogy of surface materials as well as the geologic processes and surface-atmosphere interactions that created and modified the surface. The instrument package will also enable scientists to determine dust particle size and water vapor abundance in the atmosphere.

🔲 Mars Pathfinder Page - information on the mission, Mars, and other resources
🔲 Mars global view showing the Viking and Mars Pathfinder landing sites
🔲 Mars Mileage Guide - distance between Pathfinder and Viking landing sites and other martian features
🔲 Mars Pathfinder Entry Strategy - the plans for Mars Pathfinder atmospheric entry and landing
🔲 NSSDC Planetary Page

Questions and comments about this page should be addressed to:
Dr. David R. Williams, dwilliam@nssdc.gsfc.nasa.gov, (301) 286-1258
NSSDC, Mail Code 633, NASA/Goddard Space Flight Center, Greenbelt, MD 20771

NSSDC National Space Science Data Center

> This Web site contains links to sites about the Mars Pathfinder mission. Click on the link to the National Space Science Data Center.

What's New in Planetary Science

Results of the Mars Pathfinder mission, including a mission summary and APXS Mars surface composition results have been published in *Science* magazine.

- The Mars Global Surveyor resumed its aerobraking activities on November 7th following an analysis of the condition of the solar panels by the project. More detail is available in the NASA press release from the press conference held on 10 November.

- The first 14 volumes of the Clementine Lunar Digital Image Model CD-ROMs are now available from NSSDC. These volumes are regional mosaics created from Clementine images showing the Moon at a resolution of 100 meters/pixel. Volume 15 has lower resolution global views and is expected at the end of 1997.

🔲 Upcoming Planetary Events and Missions
🔲 New and Incoming Planetary Data at NSSDC
🔲 New and Updated Planetary Pages

> This Web site contains links to sites that have broader information about space exploration. Click on the link to Upcoming Planetary Events and Missions.

Upcoming Planetary Events and Missions

Upcoming Planetary Launches and Events

1997 December 16 - Galileo - Europa closest flyby

1998 January 6 - **Lunar Prospector** - Launch of NASA Global Orbiter Mission to the Moon
1998 January 23 - NEAR - Earth Flyby
1998 April 26 - Cassini - Venus-1 Flyby
1998 July - New Millenium Deep Space-1 - Launch of NASA Flyby Mission to Asteroid 3352 McAuliffe and Comet
P/West-Kohoutek-Ikemura
1998 August 6 - **Planet-B** - Launch of ISAS (Japan) Orbiter Mission to Mars
1998 December - **Mars Surveyor '98 Orbiter** - Launch of NASA Orbiter Mission to Mars

> Click on Cassini link to go to a Web site that deals with a project to explore Saturn.

Cassini

Cassini has launched!

Launch Date/Time: 15 October 1997 at 08:43 UTC
Launch Vehicle: Titan IV-Centaur
Planned on-orbit mass: 2175 Kg
Power System: Radioisotope Thermal Generators (RTGs) of 630 W

The Cassini Orbiter's mission consists of delivering a probe (called Huygens, provided by ESA) to Titan, and then remaining in orbit around Saturn for detailed studies of the planet and its rings and satellites. The principal objectives are to: (1) determine the three-dimensional structure and dynamical behavior of the rings; (2) determine the composition of the satellite surfaces and

- This is the stream of consciousness method of searching the Internet (**surfing**). It may be interesting and fun to locate information this way, but there are drawbacks. Surfing randomly for information is time consuming and the results are frequently inconsistent and incomplete. It can also be expensive if you are charged fees for connect time to your Internet Service Provider.

- If you want a more systematic and organized way of looking for information, you can connect to one of several search sites that use **search engines** to track, catalog, and index information on the Internet.

Search Sites

- A **search site** builds its catalog using a search engine. A search engine is a software program that goes out on the Web, seeking Web sites, and cataloging them, usually by downloading their home pages.

- Search sites are classified by the way they gather Web site information. All search sites use a search engine in one way or another to gather information. Below is an explanation of how the major search services assemble and index information.

Search Engines

- A search site builds its catalog using a **search engine**. A search engine is a software program that goes out on the Web, seeking Web sites, and cataloging them, usually by downloading their home pages.

- Search engines are sometimes called **spiders** or **crawlers** because they crawl the Web.

- Search engines constantly visit sites on the Web to create catalogs of Web pages and keep them up to date.

- Major search engines include: **AltaVista**, **HotBot**, **Open Text**.

Directories

- Search **directories** catalog information by building hierarchical indexes. Since humans assemble the catalogs, information is often more relevant than the indexes that are assembled by Web crawlers. Directories may be better organized than search engine sites, but they will not be as complete or up-to-date as search engines that constantly check for new material on the Internet.

- **Yahoo**, the oldest search service on the World Wide Web, is the best example of Internet search directories. Other major search directories are: **Infoseek**, **Magellan**, **Lycos**.

Multi-Threaded Search Engines

- Another type of search engine, called a **multi-threaded** search engine, searches other Web search sites and gathers the results of these searches for your use.

- Because they search the catalogs of other search sites, multi-threaded search sites do not maintain their own catalogs. These search sites provide more search options than subject-and-keyword search sites, and they typically return more specific information with further precision. However, multi-threaded search sites are much slower to return search results than subject-and-keyword search sites.

- Multi-threaded search sites include **SavvySearch** and **Internet Sleuth**.

- If you are using Internet Explorer or Netscape Navigator, you can click on the Search button on the toolbar to access a number of search services.

Search Basics

■ When you connect to a search site, the home page has a text box for typing the words you want to use in your search. These words are called a **text string**. The text string may be a single word or phrase, or it may be a complex string which uses **operators** to modify the search (see "Search Engines: 21" for more information on operators). Illustrated below is the opening page of Yahoo, one of the oldest and most popular search directories.

Click to initiate search.

Links to Yahoo categories

Access options to refine search.

Regional links

Yahoo! Mail
free email

Shop and Win @ NetBuyer

Win a Sports
Dream Trip

Search   options

Yellow Pages - People Search - Maps - Classifieds - Personals - Chat - **Email**
Holiday Shopping - My Yahoo! - News - Sports - Weather - Stoc

- **Arts and Humanities**
  Architecture, Photography, Literature...

- **Business and Economy [Xtra!]**
  Companies, Finance, Employment...

- **Computers and Internet [Xtra!]**
  Internet, WWW, Software, Multimedia...

- **Education**
  Universities, K-12, College Entrance...

- **Entertainment [Xtra!]**
  Cool Links, Movies, Music, Humor...

- **Government**
  Military, Politics [Xtra!], Law, Taxes...

- **Health [Xtra!]**
  Medicine, Drugs, Diseases, Fitness...

- **News and Media [**
  Current Events, Magazines, TV, Newspapers...

- **Recreation and Sports [Xtra!]**
  Sports, Games, Travel, Autos, Outdoors...

- **Reference**
  Libraries, Dictionaries, Phone Numbers...

- **Regional**
  Countries, Regions, U.S. States...

- **Science**
  CS, Biology, Astronomy, Engineering...

- **Social Science**
  Anthropology, Sociology, Economics...

- **Society and Culture**
  People, Environment, Religion...

Yahooligans! for Kids - Beatrice's Guide - MTV/Yahoo! unfURLed - Yahoo! Internet Life
What's New - Weekly Picks - Today's Web Events
Visa Shopping Guide - Yahoo! Store

World Yahoos Australia & NZ - Canada - Denmark - France - Germany - Japan - Korea
Norway - SE Asia - Sweden - UK & Ireland
Yahoo! Metros Atlanta - Austin - Boston - Chicago - Dallas / Fort Worth - Los Angeles
Get Local Miami - Minneapolis / St. Paul - New York - S.F. Bay - Seattle - Wash D.C.

Smart Shopping with **VISA**

How to Suggest a Site - Company Info - Openings at Yahoo! - Contributors - Yahoo! to Go

- Once you have entered a text string, initiate the search by either pressing the Enter key or by clicking on the search button. This button may be called Search, Go Get It, Seek Now, Find, or something similar.
- For the best search results:
  - Always check for misspelled words and typing errors.
  - Use descriptive words and phrases.
  - Use synonyms and variations of words.
  - Find and follow the instructions that the search site suggests for constructing a good search.
  - Eliminate unnecessary words (the, a, an, etc.) from the search string. Concentrate on key words and phrases.
  - Test your search string on several different search sites. Search results from different sites can vary greatly.
  - Explore some of the sites that appear on your initial search and locate terms that would help you refine your search string.

Search Engines: 20

◆ Simple Searches ◆ Refine a Search ◆ Get Help

Simple Searches

- Searches can be simple or complex, depending on how you design the search string in the text box.

- A **simple search** uses a text string, usually one or two key words, to search for matches in a search engine's catalog. A simple search is the broadest kind of search.

  - The key words may be specific, such as Internet Explorer browser, current stock quotes, or Macintosh computers, or they may be general, such as software, economy, or computer.

  - The catalog search will return a list, typically quite large, of Web pages and URLs whose descriptions contain the text string you want to find. Frequently these searches will yield results with completely unrelated items.

- When you start a search, the Web site searches its catalog for occurrences of your text string. (Some search sites don't have their own catalog, so they search the catalogs of other search sites.) The results of the search, typically a list of Web sites whose descriptions have words that match your text string are displayed in the window of your browser.

- Each search site has its own criteria for rating the matches of a catalog search and setting the order in which they are displayed.

- The catalog usually searches for matches of the text string in the URLs of Web sites. It also searches for key words, phrases, and meta-tags (key words that are part of the Web page, but are not displayed in a browser) in the cataloged Web pages.

- The information displayed on the results page will vary, depending on the search and display options selected and the search site you are using. The most likely matches for your text string appear first in the results list, followed by other likely matches on successive pages.

  √ There may be thousands of matches that contain the search string you specified. The matches are displayed a page at a time. You can view the next page by clicking on the "next page" link provided at the bottom of each search results page.

- For example, if you do a search on the word *Greek*, you'll get results, as illustrated below, that display links to a wide range of links that have something to do with Greek. Note the number of documents that contain the search word.

√ *These examples use AltaVista to perform the search. Your results may vary with other search tools.*

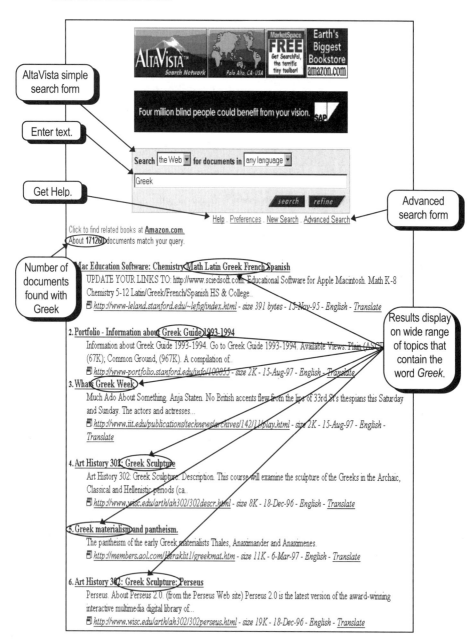

AltaVista simple search form

Enter text.

Get Help.

Number of documents found with Greek

Advanced search form

Results display on wide range of topics that contain the word *Greek.*

- You can scan the displayed results to see if a site contains the information you are looking for. Site names are clickable links. After visiting a site, you can return to the search site by clicking the Back button on your browser. You can then choose a different site to visit or perform another search.

Refine a Search

- Suppose that you only want to view links that deal with Greek *tragedies*. The natural inclination would be to enter Greek tragedies in the search string to reduce the number of documents that the search tool finds. Note, however, the number of documents that were found when Greek tragedies was entered in this search. Since the search string didn't include a special operator to tell the search engine to look for sites that contain both Greek *and* tragedies, the results display sites that contain Greek *OR* tragedies in addition to sites that contain Greek *AND* tragedies.

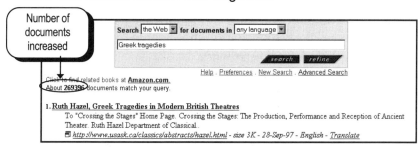

- To reduce the number of documents in this search, enter *Greek* press space once, then enter a plus sign (+) and the word tragedies (Greek +tragedies) then click Search. This tells AltaVista to look for articles that contain Greek *and* tragedies in the documents. Note the results that display when the plus is added to the search.

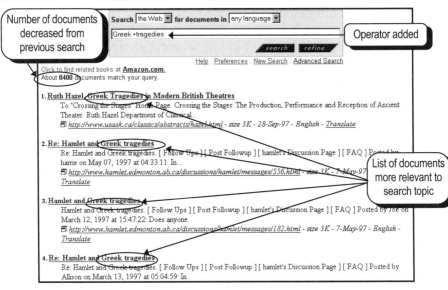

Number of documents decreased from previous search

Operator added

List of documents more relevant to search topic

- The number of documents listed is dramatically reduced, and the documents displayed display information that is more closely related to the topic, Greek tragedies.

- You can also *exclude* words by using the minus sign (-) to further refine a search and eliminate unwanted documents in the results. For example, if you wanted to find articles about Greek tragedies but not ones that deal with Hamlet, enter a search string like this: *Greek +tragedies -Hamlet*. Note the different results that display:

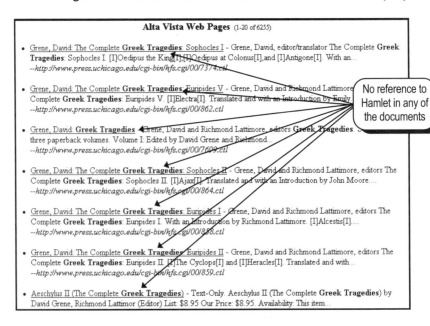

No reference to Hamlet in any of the documents

Get Help

- Check the Help features on the search tool that you are using to see what operators are available. Since there are no standards governing the use of operators, search sites can develop their own. Illustrated on the page 99 are samples of the help available for performing a simple search in AltaVista and Yahoo.

AltaVista Help for Simple Searches

Natural Language queries: (always try this first)

Type a word or phrase or a question (for example, **weather Boston** or **what is the weather in Boston?**), then click Search (or press the Enter key). If the information you want from this sort of query isn't on the first couple of pages, try adding a few more specific words.

Requiring/Excluding Words:

Often you will know a word that will be guaranteed to appear in a document for which you are searching. If this is the case, require that the word appear in all of the results by attaching a "+" to the beginning of the word (for example, to find an article on pet care, you might try the query **dog cat pet +care**). You may also find that when you search on a vague topic, you get a very broad set of results. You can quickly reject results by adding a term that appears often in unwanted articles with a "-" before it (for example, to find a recipe for oatmeal raisin cookies without nuts try **oatmeal raisin cookie -nut* -walnut***).

Exact Phrases:

If you know that a certain phrase will appear on the page you are looking for, put the phrase in quotes. (for example, try entering song lyrics such as **"you ain't nothing but a hound dog"**)

Yahoo Help for Simple Searches

Tips for Better Searching

- **Use Double Quotes Around Words that are Part of a Phrase**

  example `"great barrier reef"` [Search]

- **Specify Words that Must Appear in the Results**
  Attach a **+** in front words that *must* appear in result documents.

  example: `sting +police` [Search]

- **Specify Words that Should Not Appear in the Results**
  Attach a **−** in front of words that *must not* appear in result documents.

  example: `python -monty` [Search]

◆ **Complex Searches** ◆ **Operators** ◆ **Boolean Operators**
◆ **Plus (+)/Minus (-) System** ◆ **Grouping Operators**
◆ **Case Sensitive** ◆ **Special Characters and Punctuation**
◆ **Major Search Engines and Operators**

Complex Searches

■ When you first connect to a search site, the temptation to type in text and hit the search button is great. Resist it. Taking time to read and understand the search rules of the site will save the time you'll waste by creating a search that yields an overwhelming number of hits. Some of what you want may be buried somewhere in that enormous list, but working your way through the irrelevant sites can waste time, cause frustration, and be very discouraging.

■ In "Search Engines: 20," you learned how simply using a plus or minus sign can create a search that gives a more pertinent list of sites. Now, you will see how to use operators to restrict and refine your searches even more.

Operators

■ A **complex search** usually contains several words in the text string including **operators** that modify the text string. Operators are words or symbols that modify the search string instead of being part of it.

■ Using operators and several descriptive words can narrow your search for information, which means the results will reduce the number of sites that display. This means the resulting list of sites should be more relevant to what you want, thereby saving you time and probably money.

■ Each search site develops its own set of restrictions and options to create searches designed to locate specific information. What follows are some of the commonly used operators and how they are used.

Boolean Operators

- **Boolean operators** specify required words, excluded words, and complex combinations of words to be found during a search. Depending on the site, Boolean operators may be represented by words or symbols.

- The most common Boolean operators are:

AND The documents found in the search must contain *all words* joined by the AND operator. For example, a search for *Microsoft* AND *Internet* AND *Explorer* will find sites which contain all three words (*Microsoft*, *Internet*, and *Explorer*).

OR The documents found in the search must contain *at least one of the words* joined by the OR operator. The documents may contain both, but this is not required. For example, a search for *Web* OR *Internet* will find sites which contain either the word *Web* or the word *Internet*.

NOT The documents found in the search must not contain the word following the NOT operator. For example, a search for *Washington* NOT *DC* will find sites which contain the word *Washington* but none about *Washington DC*.

NEAR The documents found in the search must contain the words joined by the NEAR operator within a specified number of words, typically ten. For example, *RAM* NEAR memory will find sites with the word *RAM* and the word *memory* within ten words of each other.

- Suppose that you can't remember the name of the earthquake that occurred during the World Series in San Francisco in 1989. If you enter relevant words in the simple search function (using the plus sign) in AltaVista, here's what you get:

Click to find related books at **Amazon.com.**
About **18368** documents match your query.

1. San Francisco Earthquakes
   San Francisco Earthquake Links. The Ring of Fire/On Shakey Ground - An Earthquake overview. 1906 Earthquake - Before and After Films. 1906 Earthquake...
   http://www.exploratorium.edu/earthquake/sf.earthquakes.html - *size 2K - 11-Oct-95 - English*

2. Why Earthquakes are Inevitable in the San Francisco Bay Area
   Latest quake info. Hazards & Preparedness. More about earthquakes. Studying Earthquakes. Whats new. Home. Why Earthquakes are Inevitable in the San...
   http://quake.wr.usgs.gov/hazprep/BayAreaInsert/inevitable.html - *size 3K - 21-Mar-97 - English*

3. Museums Reach Out With Web Catalogs of Collections /WW November 4 1996
   Museums Reach Out With Web Catalogs of Collections. By Susan Moran. Earthquakes chase or keep many people away from California. The violent quake of 1989..
   http://www.webweek.com/96Nov04/markcomm/arts_sake.html - *size 9K - 17-Apr-97 - English*

4. $A History of California Earthquakes (1 of 101)
   Content Next. A History of California Earthquakes (Image 1 of 101) Earthquakes in the San Francisco Bay Region. Hayward, 1868. Vacaville, 1892. San...

Results do not answer the question.

- The results display several links to articles about earthquakes in the San Francisco area. If you click on one of these, you may find the earthquake you are looking for.

- Now examine the results of a more complex search using the same words, but using some of the advanced search options available in AltaVista. Entering the search string in the advanced search form of AltaVista displays the following:

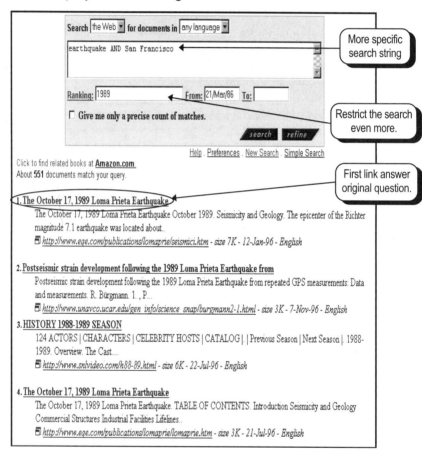

- Use the Advanced search function when you have a specific complex search string; otherwise, use the simple search function. AltaVista will automatically rank the order of the search results when you use the simple search function. When you use the advanced search function, you control the ranking of the results by entering additional search criteria in the Ranking box on the Advanced search form.

Plus (+)/Minus (-) System

■ Boolean logic is the basis for the plus and minus system of constructing a search. If the plus/minus sign is not included in the search string, the search engine assumes that you are using OR. That's why when you searched for *Greek tragedies*, AltaVista looked for documents containing either *Greek* or *tragedies*.

Plus sign (+)   Placed immediately in front of a word (no space between the plus sign and the word) means that all documents found must contain that word. (This is similar to the Boolean AND function.) For example, note the results of a search for articles about earthquakes in California, using a search string like this: *earthquakes +California*.

Click to find related books at **Amazon.com**.
About **59247** documents match your query.

1. **$A History of California Earthquakes (5 of 101)**
   Content Previous Next. A History of California Earthquakes (Image 5 of 101) Earthquake damage in San Francisco Bay Region.
   http://www.johnmartin.com/eqshow/cah_0105.htm - *size 399 bytes* - *5-Dec-96* - *English*

2. **$A History of California Earthquakes (2 of 101)**
   Content Previous Next. A History of California Earthquakes (Image 2 of 101) State map with major fault systems.
   http://www.johnmartin.com/eqshow/cah_0102.htm - *size 389 bytes* - *5-Dec-96* - *English*

3. **Earthquakes in California**
   EARTHQUAKES IN CALIFORNIA. California is the highest earthquake risk area in the contiguous United States. Several large, well-known active faults run...
   http://www.eqe.com/publications/homeprep/eqkesca.htm - *size 4K* - *26-Nov-95* - *English*

4. **$A History of California Earthquakes (16 of 101)**
   Content Previous Next. A History of California Earthquakes (Image 16 of 101) Earthquake damage during the 1957 Daly City earthquake.
   http://www.johnmartin.com/eqshow/cah_0116.htm - *size 411 bytes* - *5-Dec-96* - *English*

5. **$A History of California Earthquakes (9 of 101)**
   Content Previous Next. A History of California Earthquakes (Image 9 of 101) Earthquake damage during the 1868 Hayward earthquake.
   http://www.johnmartin.com/eqshow/cah_0109.htm - *size 407 bytes* - *5-Dec-96* - *English*

Minus sign (-)   Place immediately in front of a word (again, no space) means that all documents found will NOT contain that word. (This is the Boolean NOT function.) For example, note the results of search for articles about earthquakes that do *not include* California using a search string like this: *earthquakes -California*.

```
Click to find related books at Amazon.com.
12985 documents match your query.

1. IGS FAQs - Earthquakes
     Q: I was born and raised in South Bend, Indiana and I remember experiencing a tremor on a Fall Saturday, right about
     mid-day, sometime between 1968 and...
     http://www.indiana.edu/~igs/faqs/faqquake.html - size 3K - 15-Jul-97 - English

2. Index of /ftp/ca.earthquakes/1994/
     Index of /ftp/ca.earthquakes/1994/ Name Last modified Size Description. Parent Directory 30-Jan-97 10:35 -
     940106.gif 16-Nov-94 14:18 11K. 940106.ps.Z...
     http://scec.gps.caltech.edu/ftp/ca.earthquakes/1994/ - size 21K - 15-Aug-97 - English

3. Index of /ftp/ca.earthquakes/1993/
     Index of /ftp/ca.earthquakes/1993/ Name Last modified Size Description. Parent Directory 30-Jan-97 10:35 -
     930107.ps.Z 08-Aug-94 10:17 40K. 930107.txt.Z...
     http://scec.gps.caltech.edu/ftp/ca.earthquakes/1993/ - size 18K - 15-Aug-97 - English

4. USENET FAQs - sci.geo.earthquakes
     USENET FAQs. sci.geo.earthquakes. FAQs in this newsgroup. Satellite Imagery FAQ - Pointer.
     http://www.cis.ohio-state.edu/hypertext/faq/usenet-faqs/bygroup/sci/geo/earthquakes/top.html - size 328 bytes
     - 15-Aug-97 - English

5. GEOL 240lxg: Earthquakes
     GEOL 240lxg: Earthquakes. Department: Earth Sciences. Instructor: Sammis, Charles & Teng, Ta-Liang. Semester
     offered: Fall Spring. Category: Natural...
     http://www.usc.edu/Library/Gede/GEOL240lxg.SammisCharles.html - size 2K - 22-Nov-95 - English
```

Grouping Operators

- The grouping **operators** join words and phrases together to be treated as a single unit or determine the order in which Boolean operators are applied.

- The most common grouping operators are:

Double quotes   The documents found in the search must contain the words inside double quotes exactly as entered. For example, a search for "*World Wide Web*" will find sites whose descriptions contain the phrase *World Wide Web*, not the individual words separated by other words or the same words uncapitalized.

Parentheses   Words and operators can be grouped to refine searches using parentheses or to define the order in which Boolean operators are applied. For example, a search for (*Internet OR Web*) AND *browser* will find sites whose descriptions contain the words *Internet* and *browser* or *Web* and *browser*. (Note that this is *not* the same search as *Internet* OR *Web AND browser*, which finds sites whose descriptions contain either the word *Internet* or both of the words *Web* and *browser*.)

Case Sensitive

■ If you enter a word using all lowercase (hamlet), some search engines will look for both upper and lower case versions of the word. If you use uppercase in the search (Hamlet), the search engine will locate documents that only use the uppercase version.

Special Characters and Punctuation

■ Special characters and punctuation can also be used to filter results in complex searches. The most widely used character, the asterisk (*) is used when a word in a search can have a number of different forms. Using the asterisk (*) as a wildcard tells the search engine to find documents that contain any form of the word. For example, if you create a search for blue*, note the wide range of documents that show up in the search results.

Click to find related books at **Amazon.com**.
About **800775** documents match your query.

1. Yahoo! - U.S. blue chips slash losses, Nasdaq edges higher
   Yahoo | Write Us | Search | Headlines | Info] [Business - Company - Industry - Finance - PR Newswire - Business Wire - Quotes] Thursday August 14 3:20..
   http://biz.yahoo.com/finance/97/08/14/z0000_21.html - size 4K - 15-Aug-97 - English

2. SI: BLUE DESERT MINING, BDE-ASE
   BLUE DESERT MINING, BDE-ASE. Carlson On-line Profile | Started By: Dale Schwartzenhauer Date: Mar 9 1997 12:52AM EST. Investors should check out BDE, one..
   http://www.techstocks.com/~wsapi/investor/Subject-13562 - size 4K - 15-Aug-97 - English

3. UBL Artist: Daly Planet Blues Band
   Daly Planet Blues Band. The Daly Planet home page The only resource for info on this jam band from Hilton Head Island, SC. Band info, pictures, contact...
   http://www.ubl.com/artists/009821.html - size 6K - 7-Aug-97 - English

4. takuroku blues
   http://www.sainet.or.jp/~akihisa/ - size 242 bytes - 16-Feb-97

5. From Deep Blue to deep space: Take a panoramic look at Mars' surface
   Take a panoramic look at Mars' surface. To view the image* below, you'll need to install IBM's PanoramIX plug-in for the Netscape Navigator browser. The...
   http://www.ibm.com/Stories/1997/07/space6.html - size 2K - 30-Jul-97 - English

---

■ Wildcards are useful if you are looking for a word that could be singular or plural (look for dog*, instead of dog to broaden the search results).

■ Other characters that can help limit, filter, and sort results include: %, $, !, | (called the piping symbol), ~ (called the tilde), < (less than), and > (greater than). Check the rules of the individual search engines to see how, or if, these characters can be used.

Major Search Engines and Operators

■ Below is a table of the major search tools and how they use some of the search operators. Be sure to check out the search tips and help sections of the sites that you use frequently to see the most current search options. Search tools are constantly updating and improving their sites in response to users' needs.

Search Tool	Boolean operators	+/–	Grouping Operators	Case Sensitivity
AltaVista	✓	✓	✓	✓
AOL NetFind	✓	✓		
Excite	✓	✓	✓	
HotBot	✓	✓	✓	✓
Infoseek		✓	✓	✓
Lycos		✓	✓	
SavvySearch		✓	✓	
Yahoo	✓	✓	✓	✓

WEB RESOURCES

Use General Sites

◆ America Online ◆ Microsoft Network ◆ Pathfinder

General sites such as America Online and Microsoft Network have become much more than gateways to the World Wide Web. The best of these sites offer rich online content that can eliminate the need to surf and search the sometimes confusing and tangled Web.

At these general sites you can find the day's news, weather, sports, opinion, special interest features, and in some cases travel services, entertainment reviews, and other specialty information. Some sites also offer you the option of tailoring the home page to suit your personal needs.

These sites are bound to improve as they compete for additional subscribers with more and better content. Take advantage of these sites to get a great start to your Web experience every time you log online.

America Online

http://www.aol.com

 The home page for the leading commercial online service provides a well-organized directory of links to dozens of top Web sites along with brief reviews of each site.

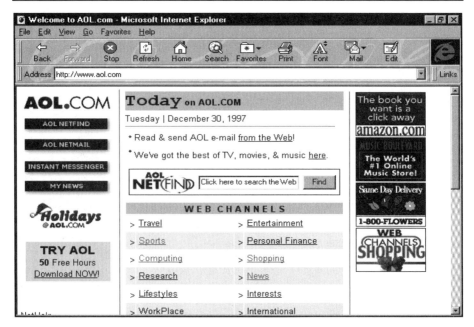

- The AOL Web site isn't just for Internet newcomers and home Web surfers. This site provides a good jumping-off point for any practical Web search.

- The AOL site has a comprehensive and well-organized Web directory, with access to dozens of links to many of the best resources available on the Web. Just click one of the AOL channels to see links to Web sites that AOL has selected as favorites along with a brief descriptive paragraph about each site.

- Though most of the channels are primarily oriented to a consumer audience, you can click the WorkPlace channel to see a very complete directory of business Web site links and associated site reviews.

- A few of the selected favorites on each channel are links to an AOL service available only to AOL members, but you will find many more links to sites available to you on the Web.

- A selection of AOL Web site reviews is arranged at the left side of each channel page. Click one of the review topics to dig down deeper and find more Web site links.

- Another nice feature at the AOL site is the easy access to search engine text boxes, where you can quickly enter a keyword search topic and click to find what you need. Each AOL channel typically showcases two or three Web sites near the top of the channel page by including search engine text boxes for those sites.

- Click the NetFind link to use the very helpful Time Savers directory. Here you will find links to Web resources for many common tasks such as Find an Airline or Hotel, Plan a Night Out, Plan a Night In, Manage Your Investments, Your Health, and Your Government.

- Links to AOL services such as NetMail (Web access e-mail) and Instant Messenger are also featured at the AOL site, but you must be an AOL member to use these services.

Microsoft Network
http://www.msn.com

 This leading computer software developer provides a broad range of online content for business and consumer research as well as entertainment.

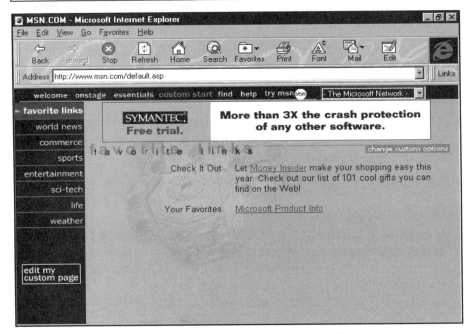

- There has been a pattern over the years when Microsoft enters a promising new market: Microsoft may not offer the first or best product, but after a while, the Microsoft product catches on and then overtakes the competition.

- The same pattern holds true in the commercial online service market. Microsoft Network (MSN) was supposed to take over the world when it was offered as an icon on the Windows 95 desktop several years ago. However, as many people who clicked the icon on their desktop found, the initial content available on MSN usually wasn't worth a second look. In addition, the network connections were typically slow and unreliable.

- Over the past couple of years, MSN's content has vastly improved, even if the network connections remain slow at times. MSN's wide range of consumer and business Web site offerings makes it well worth a stop on your online search.

- Topping the list of MSN sites is the award winning Expedia travel service. (See "Plan and Book Travel Online.") Expedia is an example of how much interactivity and rich content can be delivered on a commercial Web site. Expedia's outstanding travel-booking wizard makes it a fine business and sales resource. Sidewalk is a wonderfully complete guide to nine U.S. cities as well as Sydney, Australia.

- Check out Microsoft Investor and Money Insider for a couple of the best investment and market sites available on the Web. Also, try the Computing Central site for computer forums, tips, software downloads, and industry news.

- The Mining Company is a new search site offered by MSN that offers the services of online guides to help you find what you want. Other MSN sites are consumer-oriented, but provide very useful and well-presented resources to help you find out about cars (CarPoint), movies (Cinemania), games (Internet Gaming Zone), music (Music Central), and shopping (Plaza).

Pathfinder

http://pathfinder.com

 Use this easy-to-access directory to find Time Warner media Web sites such as Time, Life, People, Fortune, CNNSI, and Travel & Leisure. Perhaps the most complete and wide-ranging collection of current information available on the Web.

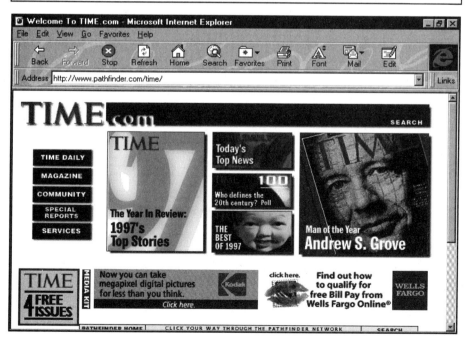

- Time Warner's Pathfinder site brings together all the news, information, and entertainment content of dozens of Web, magazine, and video properties owned by the media conglomerate.

- This site is a great source for news, sports, politics, and entertainment coverage, offering links to Time, CNNSI, People, Entertainment Weekly, Variety Netwire, Life, and AllPolitics.

- The above list is just a sampling of the interesting and informative resources available at Pathfinder. You can also find financial sites such as Fortune, Hoover's Business Resources, Money Daily, Money Online, Portfolio Tracker, and Quick Quotes.

- Get travel news and fares at the Travel & Leisure, WebFlyer, PlanetSurfer, and Magellan Maps sites. Net Culture sites feature PC and Web news and information.

- If you want to shop, click on one of the many Marketplace sites, including BarnesandNoble.com, CDNow, Fortune Book Fair, Internet Shopping Network, and Time Life Photo Sight.

- Pathfinder also provides free e-mail service, a financial calculator, community chat sites, a cyberdating service, and an investment portfolio tracker. This wide-ranging collection of sites may be one of the most comprehensive information sources available on the Web.

Use Directories and Search Engines

◆ **Yahoo!** ◆ **Excite** ◆ **Dogpile** ◆ **Open Text** ◆ **Other Sites**

If you're using the Internet for business, your main objective for being online is most likely to find a particular piece of information. Although it can be a lot of fun, you don't want to waste time surfing the Web.

When you want information on the Web fast but don't know where to look, the best place to start is a directory or search engine. These sites help organize the vast contents of the Internet and the World Wide Web so that you can focus your search efforts and zoom to the exact Web site (or other Internet service) you need.

Directories Organize the Web

- Though they go about it in different ways, directories and search engines have the same goal—locating information online. Directories provide a map of how information is organized on the World Wide Web. Typically, they break the Web down into a number of categories—usually numbering about a dozen or so.

- Categories might include broad search areas such as Arts and Humanities, Business, Computers and Internet, News and Media, Science, and Entertainment. Beyond the main categories, directories typically break Web contents down into finer and finer subcategories. For example, the Business category might be split into Companies, Investing, Classifieds, Taxes, and more. Searching these layers of subcategories until you find what you need is called "drilling down" in the directory.

Search Engines Comb the Web

- Search engines provide you with readily accessible database search software that searches Web contents or, in some cases, directories or indexes of Web contents. You enter one or more keywords into the search engine's text box, click a button on screen, and then let the software do the work.

- Typically, a search engine will return a listing of results that match your keyword(s) as closely as possible. Many search engines include confidence rankings that indicate how closely the software thinks each result matches your keyword(s). Results may be links to Web sites or links to directory categories or subcategories.

- Search Web sites can include directories, search engines, or both. They may also contain news updates and other content found only at the search site. Each of these sites finds information on the Web differently, and that can help you find what you need faster once you have learned the unique benefits of each site's approach.

Yahoo!

http://www.yahoo.com

 Yahoo!, the original Web search site, provides a well-organized directory of Web contents, a powerful search engine, and an ever-growing list of new features that focus on special interests.

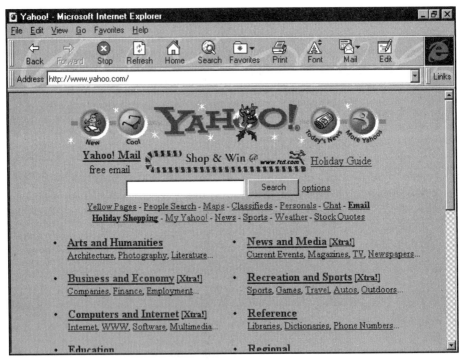

- Perhaps the most recognizable name in the Web searching business is Yahoo!, the granddaddy of them all. The site is continuously updated and new Yahoo! services are added regularly to expand the site. Click on the New icon at the top of the home page to see what features have been added recently.

- What Yahoo! does best is organize the Web. The list of directory categories and subcategories on the Yahoo! home page has been emulated by many other Web search and directory sites. If you have a fairly good idea of what you're looking for, click the category (or subcategory) link that comes closest to matching your interest.

- After clicking a category link, you will see a page of subcategory links. Click one of these to drill down even further in the directory structure and narrow your search. After two or three clicks, you should start to zero in on links to specific Web sites.

- You can also click on the Indices link after you have clicked a top-level category link to see a listing of Web sites that serve as link directories for that particular topic. For example, click Business and Economy, then click Indices to see links to sites such as All Business Network, Business Sense, and Business Sources on the Net.

- From the Yahoo! home page you can also click Today's News icon for a quick way to check the day's headlines. Click the More Yahoos icon to see a listing of other Yahoo! services such as My Yahoo! (where you can customize the site to your liking), Get Local (focusing on a Zip Code you specify), Yahoo! Chat (for online talk), and various Yahoo! Metros (focusing on major cities across the country). Click the home page Cool icon to see a directory of more off-the-wall Web site categories.

- You can also search the Yahoo! directories by entering a keyword(s) in the search text boxes available on every page. You can search the entire Yahoo! directory or limit the search to the portion you're currently visiting. Remember, Yahoo! searches only its directories, which consist of Web page titles and descriptions, not the full Web. This yields more focused search results.

Excite

http://www.excite.com

 Excite features a tight directory structure and allows searching by concepts, which means you can enter conversational search phrases and get more targeted results.

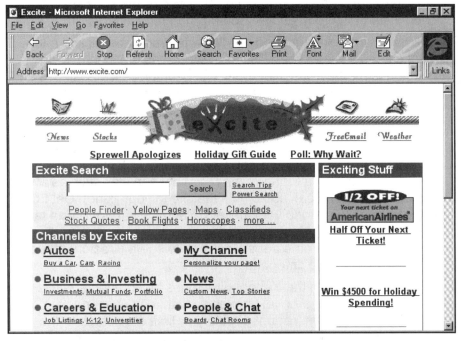

- After trying a few keyword searches, you may come to discover that Web search engines take your keywords very literally. The Excite Web site attempts to solve this problem by enabling you to search by concepts instead of by keywords.

- That is, the Excite search engine knows that words such as "coffee" and "cake" can have different meanings when they are used together from when they are used separately. The Excite engine also knows that words such as "play" can have many meanings, and it takes these into account when you enter a concept phrase.

- The bottom line is that you can use conversational phrases to describe what you want Excite to find. For example, if you're looking for plays by Arthur Miller, just type in "plays by Arthur Miller." If you're looking for sports plays of the day, just type in "sports plays of the day." Excite eliminates the process of deciding what the best keyword strategy will be to get the search results you want.

116

- Excite also provides a very tight Web directory that includes only three levels of categories. This is a reflection of the more narrow criteria Excite uses to screen sites indexed in its directory.

- You are guaranteed to find links to Web sites by the time you click three Excite category links. You can also read Excite summaries of each site that links to it. The net result for you is a quicker, more informed directory search than you can perform at other directory sites.

- Excite also includes links to features such as News (well-organized directory of wire service reports), Stocks (a business news summary page with stock quotes), TV (a table-style television guide), and Weather (national and local forecasts).

Dogpile

http://www.dogpile.com

 Use this search engine of search engines to look for what you want on 25 Internet search and directory sites.

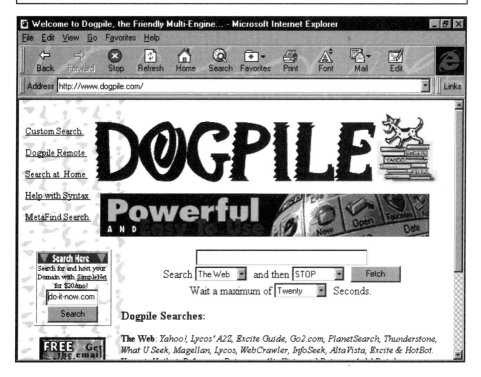

- Want to get the maximum coverage for your search? If you have trouble finding results at one search or directory site and have to jump to another, try Dogpile instead. Dogpile is the Internet search site that checks all the other important search and directory sites.

- You can enter a keyword search into the Dogpile home page and specify whether you want Dogpile to search the Web, FTP, Usenet, or newswires. You can choose to search a maximum of two of the above and then select a maximum time you want to wait for the search to be completed.

- Click the Fetch button and the powerful Dogpile search engine begins searching your selected Internet services three at a time. Dogpile searches 25 different services, including Yahoo!, Excite, Lycos, WebCrawler, InfoSeek, AltaVista, HotBot, DejaNews, and more. You can rest assured that you have thoroughly combed the Internet after finishing a Dogpile search.

- You can also specify the order in which you want Dogpile to search by clicking on the Custom Search link. Just select the service you want to search for each spot on the Dogpile search list from 1 to 25.

- Click on the Help with Syntax link to read a detailed how-to page for using keyword search operators such as AND, OR, NOT, and NEAR. Because some search engines support these keyword operators in different ways, you should check out the Help with Syntax page before constructing any complex Dogpile searches.

Open Text

http://index.opentext.net

 Search every word of the World Wide Web with the Open Text engine.

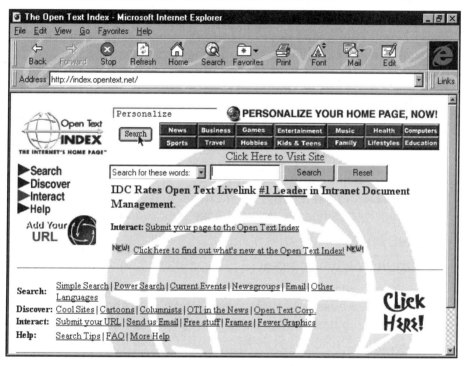

- When you really want to search the entire World Wide Web, use the Open Text search engine. Open Text treats the Web as one gigantic text file. Your keyword search in Open Text is virtually the same as using the Find feature in a word processing document, but in this case the document is the Web.

- From the Open Text index page, enter your keyword search in the text box. Click on the search button and wait for a results page to appear.

- Typically, you will get a large number of pages that match your search keyword(s). You can narrow the search by clicking the Power Search link. On the Power Search page you can enter multiple search keywords (one per text box), select where you want to search (narrow the search to titles, summaries, first headings, or

URLs), and link the keywords with search operators such as and, or, but not, near, or followed by.

- Drop-down list menus in Power Search provide choices for search locations and operators to make selection easier. Remember that the more keywords you use, the narrower your search will be (unless you connect the words with or, which includes all the keywords).

- You can also search current events, e-mail, newsgroups, and other languages. With a little practice and experimentation, Open Text searches can yield pleasantly surprising and highly effective search results.

Other Sites

Infoseek

http://www.infoseek.com

- Search any part of the Web quickly and easily with this widely respected search and directory page. It is easy to perform quick searches as well more complex searches at this site.

Lycos

http://www.lycos.com

- This full-featured search and directory site is famous for its top 5% reviews of Web sites. Its high-powered Custom Search page lets you hone in on the results you need.

DejaNews

http://www.dejanews.com

- This site searches Usenet newsgroups, the Internet's version of online chat bulletin boards. Handy for finding experts on a particular topic or just tapping into a discussion about a subject of interest.

The Mining Company

http://www.miningcompany.com

- This site takes a unique approach to finding information on the Web, with special interest sections led by "Guides" who specialize in a particular topic area. The Guide points you to links of interest, and you can also search the site by interest areas, subsections, or related sites.

Check Business News

◆ BusinessWeek Online ◆ Forbes Digital Tool ◆ Journal of Commerce
◆ Upside.Com ◆ Other Sites

Check these sites to get a handle on business news and trends. Though there are a multitude of online sites for business magazines, journals, and newspapers, all the sites featured here combine complete coverage, timely updates, and in-depth reporting. Features and opinion pieces provide you with expert analysis to aid in business decision making.

BusinessWeek Online

http://www.businessweek.com

 The online home of this top business weekly magazine provides in-depth coverage of the week's events as well as a complete daily business news update.

■ BusinessWeek is a leading source of information for business people, and its online site delivers all the information you will find in the weekly magazine and then some. Though all of the BusinessWeek site is available online free of charge at the time of this writing, the editors of the magazine have announced that there will be a subscription fee starting in January 1998.

- The home page features articles from the current week's edition of the magazine. Click the picture of the magazine's cover to see a complete directory of links to the issue's contents.

- Click the BW Daily link to get a complete look at the day's business news at the Daily Briefing page. The Daily Briefing includes numerous in-depth articles produced by BusinessWeek and Standard & Poor's.

- Click on the BW Plus link to access several months' worth of archived articles on topics such as the best business schools, business books online, The Computer Room, Enterprise Online for entrepreneurs and small business owners, Investor's Central, and Personal Business.

Forbes Digital Tool

http://www.forbes.com

 Irreverent approach to commentary on the world of business makes this site a can't-miss resource.

- Forbes Magazine has long been noted for a somewhat irreverent mix of business news reporting and opinionated features and opinion pieces. You can browse the content of five Forbes publications online at the Forbes Digital Tool Web site.

- Publications available online include the original Forbes Magazine, Forbes ASAP (focused on the impact of technology in business), Forbes FYI (features, entertainment, and opinion), American Heritage (a lively magazine about American history), and the Gilder Telecosm Series (articles excerpted from the book Telecosm, which examines and predicts trends in the online world).

- As if access to all of these publications were not enough, you can also click on the Toolbox icon to use the many Forbes lists of corporations and business people (such as The 500 Largest Private Companies in the US and Corporate America's Most Powerful People), Digital Tool Databases (such as a New York dining guide and a fitness guide), cool software downloads (such as the NBD Daily Rocket Investment Monitor), and a couple of nifty financial calculators.

- You can also click the On My Mind icon to participate in an active and entertaining online forum. The Forbes Toolbox is available free of charge, for the moment at least, so stop here to get business news and views with a healthy dose of attitude.

Journal of Commerce

http://www.joc.com

 Hardcore news, facts, and figures about the marketplace, commodities, trade, and transportation.

- The Journal of Commerce (JOC) Web site keeps you up to date with trade, transportation, and global market news.
- The site has a tight focus on domestic and international commerce, including in-depth information on transportation, logistics, imports and exports, foreign markets, energy, insurance, and finance. You can also find professional reporting unique to the Journal of Commerce site on electronic communications, chemicals, and commodities.
- Check the JOC home page for commerce headlines, summaries, and links to full stories. Click the JOC News icon to go to a directory of links to top commerce news stories. Major news categories include Page One, Trade, Transportation, Insurance, Energy/Commodities, and Opinion. These links can also be found on the home page.
- You can also click to find oil prices, shipping schedules, and transportation data. The JOC is by far the most complete site for tracking the nuts and bolts of commerce and trade.

Upside.Com

http://www.upside.com

 The Upside.com site helps provide perspective on developments in business and technology.

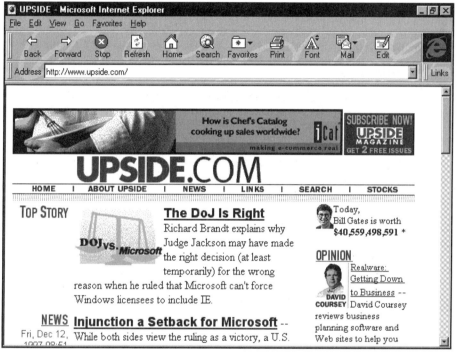

- Upside is a business magazine that focuses on industries that use and develop digital technology. The Upside.com Web site features the magazine's editorial content plus daily news updates, a technology stock watch that tracks long-term performance, as well as other tools for managers involved in the business of technology.

- Daily tech news headlines are featured at the site home page. Click the News link to scan the full text of the daily news articles. Click Links to access a number of other helpful business sites.

- The most valuable part of the Upside.com site is perhaps the wealth of insightful opinion pieces available. Click on Opinion to see a complete listing of recent columns and links to archives of past issues. The columns here are an indispensable resource for understanding the evolving future of business and technology.

Other Sites

Wall Street Journal Interactive

http://interactive.wsj.com

- For about $50 a year you get complete Wall Street Journal coverage online plus Barron's online market commentary, the SmartMoney Interactive online investment planning service, and the Briefing Book company reports database.

Inc. Online

http://www.inc.com

- The online version of Inc. magazine has been awarded the Folio editorial excellence award for best online magazine of the year. Go here for excellent features about what it takes to run a successful business and some powerful interactive worksheets that can help you analyze your company's performance.

Fast Company

http://www.fastcompany.com/today/central.html

- Innovative Web site that aspires to provide a handbook for the changing business world of new technology, global markets, and independent agents who have given up the corporate world to strike out on their own. News and features address issues for the self-employed and entrepreneurs to help smooth out the bumps in the road to success.

Red Herring

http://www.herring.com

- Another top site for business technology news and features, Red Herring also covers the business of entertainment. True to its name, Red Herring seeks to provide insight that takes you beyond technology marketing hype.

Receive Custom Information from Push Channels

◆ **PointCast** ◆ **Marimba Castanet** ◆ **NewsHound** ◆ **Other Sites**

Push technology has received a lot of press coverage in the past year as the next, or perhaps first, "killer application" for the World Wide Web. The idea is to have a customized selection of "channels" that deliver a steady stream of information to your computer's desktop over the Internet.

While the idea of having continuously and readily available information on your computer about topics of interest to you may sound like a good one, some drawbacks still exist, primarily due to the speed limitations of sending "live" information over the Internet and the fact that a stream of incoming data can slow computers and networks to a crawl.

Still, there are some definite advantages to tailoring news and information from the Web to fit your needs. The sites listed here take somewhat different approaches to delivering the information to you, using more or less intrusive means of giving you what you want. Take your hardware system and your information needs into consideration when deciding which of these services is the right one for you.

If you get ambitious, you can even use sites such as PointCast and Marimba Castanet to publish your own push channel information.

PointCast

http://www.pointcast.com

 Use this top push service to get news and business information from sources you choose delivered directly to your desktop.

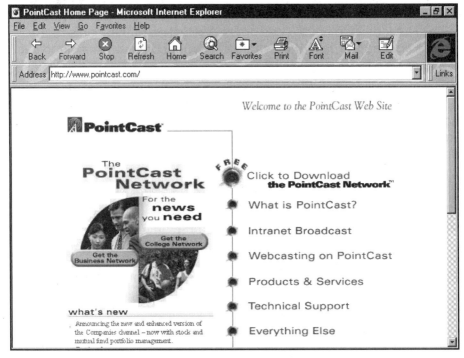

- Use the PointCast network to have information you want downloaded to your desktop automatically. The PointCast newscast gathers stories from a wide range of sources and presents them to your desktop using tickers and "smartscreens" that flash on your desktop.

- PointCast has received a lot of rave reviews over the past year for being a screen saver that keeps you on top of your world. It can, however, create information overload. Also, be aware that using PointCast can really slow down your network or computer.

- Click to read a full story or customize the channels you want to see. You can have PointCast continually update if you're directly connected to the Internet, or you can schedule times for PointCast to log on and update automatically.

- Use the Business Network to focus on daily business news. Track firms in your investment portfolio or competing companies via the Companies channel. You can also create your own push channel for broadcast on the Web using PointCast Connections.

Marimba Castanet

http://www.marimba.com

 Use Marimba Castanet to publish and to receive push channel information. Marimba's publishing tools make creating your own push channel fairly painless.

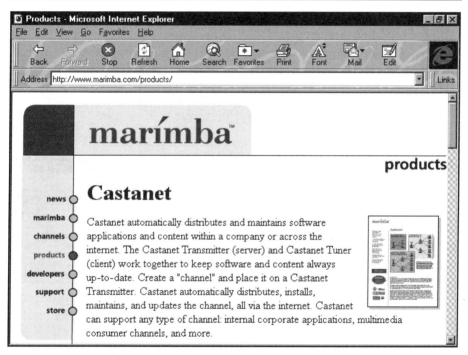

- Marimba Castanet is another popular push service that lets you download various Castanet channels of your choice and then have those channels automatically update with fresh information. You can also choose to update each time you log on to the Internet if you're not directly connected.

- Choose the channels you want to use and then customize these channels to your liking. Once you download the Castanet Tuner to your computer, you can choose any channel you want from the Castanet Transmitter.

- Channels update automatically (even when you are offline) and transmit only new information to improve the speed with which the information downloads. Once you add a channel to your computer, it is always available, whether or not you are online. You can even access the channel from your laptop while traveling and away from a network connection.

- You can also publish your own channel with Castanet fairly easily. In simplest terms, the process involves uploading the files you want to include for broadcast to the Castanet Transmitter server. Publishing it on the Transmitter server makes it available to Castanet clients as a channel that will be updated automatically on their computers each time you make a change to the channel content.

NewsHound

http://www.newshound.com

 Use a trainable search agent to track down news and information from the Web.

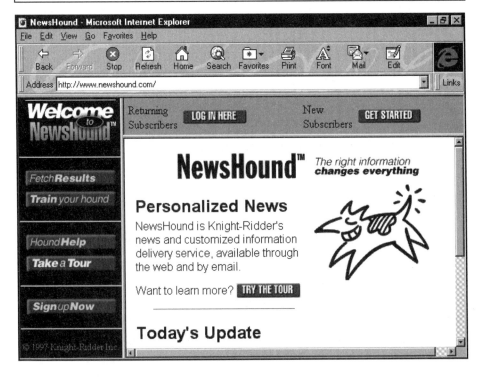

- If you want to have a push site actually track down information on the Web about a particular topic you're interested in, NewsHound delivers the goods.

- A service of the Knight-Ridder newspaper chain, NewsHound tracks and delivers up to five news or information topics for about $8 per month.

- To use NewsHound, sign up for the basic service, then "train" your NewsHounds to search for the information you want. The NewsHound service will then keep an eye out for stories and Web information that fit your search profile, gather anything that matches, and send it to your machine either in Web or e-mail format.

- This is a great way to keep tabs on a particular company, market, or developing news or technology story without the intrusiveness and system slow-downs of other push services.

Other Sites

Headliner

http://www.headliner.com

- This news and information ticker service slows your machine with a lot of graphics. However, Headliner is not as intrusive as some of the better known services such as PointCast.

Infobeat

http://www.infobeat.com

- Infobeat provides another way to avoid slowing your desktop with information you may not need. With Infobeat, you select the type of "Beats" you want to keep track of, including Finance, Sports, News, Weather, Entertainment, and more. Then Infobeat sends you personalized e-mail updates on the topics you choose.

CNN Custom News

http://www.cnn.com

- Tailor news delivery from CNN by clicking on the Custom News icon at the CNN home page. You can create a custom user profile to have news, sports scores, stock tickers—whatever information is important to you—delivered to your desktop. You can build your own profile or choose from among six Quickstart profiles including A Little of Everything, US & World News, Business, Science & Technology, Sports, as well as Lifestyle & Showbiz.

Get Breaking News with Live Newsfeeds

◆ **AP Wire Service Online** ◆ **Bloomberg** ◆ **PR Newswire** ◆ **Other Sites**

When you have to have an up-to-the-minute check of the day's top news stories, a regular news Web site just may not give you what you need. Check these news wire Web sites for coverage of the day's events updated several times an hour.

AP Wire Service Online

http://www.nytimes.com/aponline/

 Browse the most current news updates available from the Associated Press, one of the world's leading wire services.

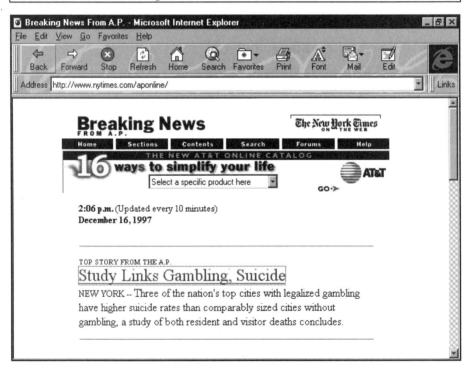

- Everyone knows the Associated Press as one of the world's leading news wire services, providing many news outlets with up-to-the-second coverage of world events as well as top-rate feature stories.

- Check the AP Breaking News page on the New York Times Web site for the most current news coverage available anywhere.

- The AP page includes a series of top headlines each followed by a brief summary. Click on the headline to read the complete article for a story.

- You may be required to register at the New York Times Web site to access the AP page, but as of this writing, the Times registration is free.

Bloomberg

http://www.bloomberg.com/welcome.html

 Click here to access the top market news and information service. The Bloomberg home page has the best presentation of the day's market activities of all Web news pages.

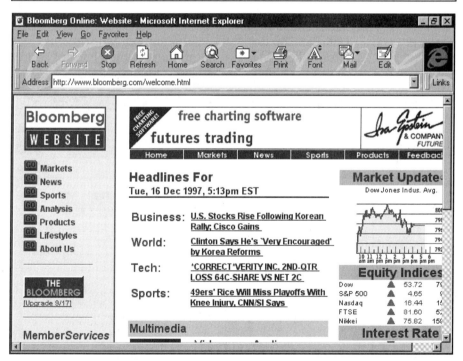

- Bloomberg L.P. provides financial and media services to more than 140,000 customers in 91 countries around the world. Perhaps best known for its market data terminals, Bloomberg's recent ventures into mass media through its cable news network and radio stations have had an immediate impact on the world news landscape.

- The Bloomberg Web site combines this focus on market services and news delivery to produce one of the best sources for up-to-the-minute business information on the Internet.

- The site's home page has the most prominent display of current market data available on a news Web site. Here you will find an hour-by-hour chart of the day's New York Stock Exchange performance along with equity indices, current 30-year interest rates, commodities, and the latest on the world's top currencies.

- Along with news headlines and summaries, a Multimedia section provides links to online feeds from the BTV cable network and the WBBR radio station. You can also click to read articles from the Bloomberg Personal magazine.

PR Newswire

http://www.prnewswire.com/

 Use this site to get the latest company news and information. Member companies submit information to the PR Newswire service for distribution.

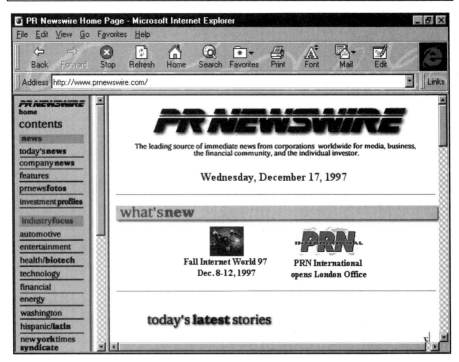

- PR Newswire has been around since 1954 as a membership association established to help company public relations professionals distribute news about their companies.

- Now PR Newswire effectively uses the World Wide Web to showcase the fine collection of industry news it gathers. Click on one of the industryfocus links at the left side of the PR Newswire home page to get breaking news about companies in specific industries or to access archives of corporate news releases and links to other industry-specific news sources online.

- Click on the Today's News link to get the latest news in one of three ways. You can click on the 100 icon to see today's 100 most recent stories or search the PR Newswire by keyword. You can also perform a more specific search for news using handy drop-down menus and selecting industry, company, ticker symbol, state, and/or subject. This is one of the most powerful search features provided by any online news page.

- Click the Company News link to see an up-to-the-minute one-year archived database of information on all companies that participate in the PR Newswire. You can search a directory of companies here or enter the company name you're looking for into a search engine text box.

- Of course, your company can also join PR Newswire to start distributing your own corporate information through the service.

Other Sites

Live Market Broadcasts

http://www.abslive.com

- Hear live stock market commentary updated every half-hour from the Atlantic Broadcast Service. You need to have the RealAudio 5.0 player software on your machine to listen in. If you don't have RealAudio 5.0 yet, you can download it free from this site.

TechWeb News

http://www.techweb.com/wire

- This technical news wire is part of the CMPNet site. CMP is the publisher of many computer and technology magazines, including Information Week, Internet Week, and Windows Magazine. The CMP site shows off the company's computer newsgathering prowess and includes links to online versions of each of its magazines.

Business Wire

http://www.businesswire.com

- This is a way to get news and information about your company *out* on the Web rather than getting news *from* the Web. For a fee, Business Wire will provide a link to your company Web page in Edgar, a link to your company listing in Hoover's Online, and a link to a company snapshot from MarketGuide, as well as post your news releases and quarterly reports. For an additional fee, Business Wire will provide audio and video file storage at your page.

- You can also send press releases via the eMail Direct service, search for information about other companies (free of charge), and browse a very complete selection of business news updated every hour (also free of charge).

Develop Sales Leads

◆ SalesLeads USA ◆ Thomas Register
◆ Forbes Annual Report on American Industry ◆ Other Sites

You can use the Web to help you develop sales leads. Many sites include searchable databases of U.S. and international corporations, including company financial information and key contacts. The large databases and powerful search engines at these sites help you quickly zero in on the types of businesses you want to find.

SalesLeads USA

http://www.lookupusa.com/

Extensive database of sales leads that you can search to find and order company information.

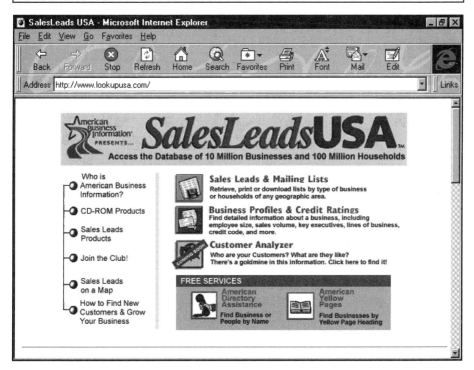

- SalesLeads USA is a Web service offered by American Business Information. The site offers a searchable database of more than 10 million businesses and more than 100 million households. Though it's hard to determine how accurate these claims and the size of the databases are, suffice to say that there is a multitude of information about prospective customers at this site. A search of businesses in just one Zip Code returned a result of more than 2,400 businesses.

- Click the Sales Leads and Mailing Lists icon to access a search engine that you can use to search by business type, state, county, metropolitan area, city, Zip Code, or by company name. After you receive initial search results, you can further narrow your search by a number of different criteria, and then choose whether you want to pay for the list of business information at the quoted price.

- Click the Business Profiles and Credit Ratings icon to search the SalesLeads USA database of company profiles. This is an excellent source of corporate information, including estimated annual sales, name of owner or top decision-maker, credit rating code, number of employees, and more. Each profile you request costs $3.

- Click on the Sales Leads products link at the home page to see a directory listing of links to each of the site's sales lead formats, including prospect lists, mailing labels, diskettes and magnetic tape, and monthly sales lead updates.

Thomas Register

http://www2.thomasregister.com/index.cgi?balancing

 Search the Thomas Register database of more than 150,000 companies free of charge. Listing your company and searching the database are both available here at no cost.

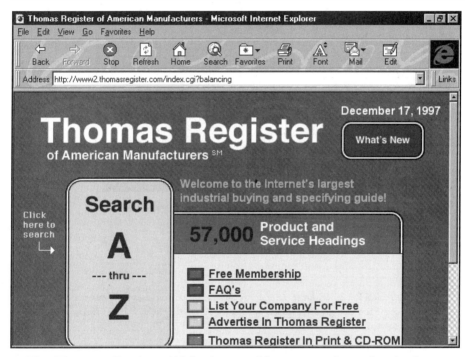

- The Thomas Register Web site provides a search engine for its database of information on more than 150,000 companies in more than 57,000 product and service headings.

- You can search the database and list your company in the database free of charge.

- The site is straightforward and easy to use. Simply click on the Search A to Z graphic, enter your ID and password, then start hunting. Site membership is free, but you have to register to search.

- The search engine is powerful, allowing you to modify search results by geographical specifications or by detailed product descriptions. You can also easily access 3,100 online supplier catalogs and links to 800 company Web sites through the Thomas Register database.

Forbes Annual Report on American Industry

http://www.forbes.com/jan1/search.htm

 Search the Forbes database of companies surveyed in its annual report on American industry. Detailed financial information on companies listed in the database is available here free of charge.

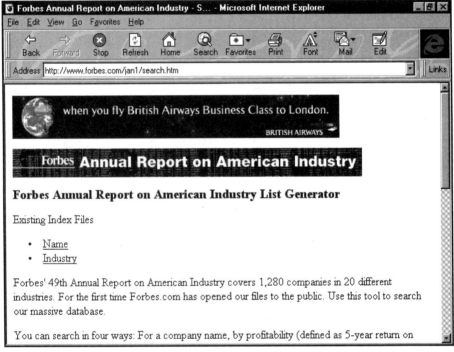

- In 1997, Forbes opened its annual report on American business and industry to the public free of charge. Use this Web site to search the database of more than 1,200 companies by name or industry.

- Click on the Industry link to see a page that has a chart breaking industries down by Profitability, Sales Growth, and Earnings Growth. Click on an industry link to see further sub-categories.

- For example, clicking on Construction takes you to a list of company links divided into the sub-categories Commercial Builders, Residential Builders, Cement and Gypsum, and Other Materials. Company links are displayed along with statistics for Five-Year Price Change, Recent Price, and EPS 1997 Estimate Dollars.

- If you already know the company you want to find, click the Name link. This takes you to an alphabetical index of the company database. Click the appropriate letter to look for the company you want. Company listings include financial information such as sales, net income, profit margin, and debt/capital ratios.

Other Sites

Dun & Bradstreet Companies Online

http://www.companiesonline.com/

- Search for information in Dun & Bradstreet's database of more than 100,000 public and private companies. The site also includes a directory listing of business categories that you can use to drill into the database to search for companies in a particular industry.

Inc. 500

http://www.inc.com/500/1997.html

- Search the Inc. magazine list of its top 500 companies. The database can be searched by company name, by descriptive keywords, by state, or by business sector.

Fortune 500

http://pathfinder.com/@@mAGEbAcAb6qkVnW7/ fortune/fortune500/500list.html

- Search a database of the most famous "500" business list of all: the Fortune 500. This page can be found at the Fortune Magazine site through the Pathfinder online service. The site is well organized, with many links that help you browse the list of companies in various ways.

Research a New Market

◆ **US Census Bureau** ◆ **University of Michigan Document Center**
◆ **FedStats** ◆ **Other Sites**

Research a target market on the Web by searching these incredibly useful sites for statistical and demographic information. Find out how many people live in a particular city, state, county, or town. Check the gender and age makeup of a certain area and find out about its economic resources. Monitor national, regional, and local economic trends, as well as business and economic trends by market sector.

US Census Bureau

http://www.census.gov

 Search for demographic and statistical information from the complete database of the U.S. Census Bureau. Easy-to-use links and directories take you to the information you need.

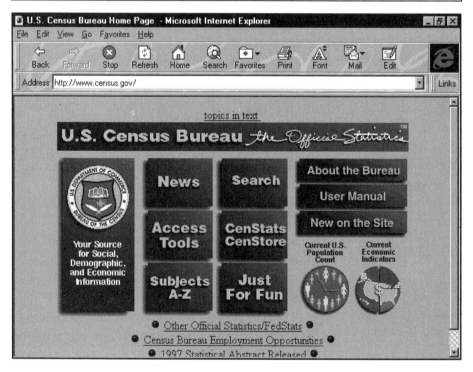

- The U.S. Census Bureau Web site is an invaluable tool for researching target market demographics. The site is well-organized and easy to use. Statistics available at this site can tell you a lot about your potential customers and how to reach them.

- A good place to start is the Current Economic Indicators icon, one of two pie-shaped links on the right of the Census home page. The link takes you to a page that includes a series of links organized into categories such as Businesses, People, and Tools and Tidbits. You can click Data Elsewhere links to find other statistical and demographic pages on the Web.

- The Businesses category includes links to various types of business and industry. The People category includes links to Income, Poverty, Labor Force, and Households. Also, be sure to check out the Census Economic Briefing Room for updates on the latest economic indicators.

- If you know exactly what you're looking for, click on the Subjects A to Z link at the Census home page. Here you will find an alphabetical index of links to Census Bureau information and statistics.

- Click on the Access Tools link at the Census home page to see a listing of tools for downloading Census information and viewing Census data online. Don't miss the Map Stats link, which takes you to an extensive gallery of interesting and useful Census Bureau maps.

University of Michigan Document Center

http://asa.ugl.lib.umich.edu/libhome/Documents.center/frames/steconfr.html

Search this vast directory and database of statistical and demographic information to research your target market. Includes dozens of links to other statistical and demographic Web sites.

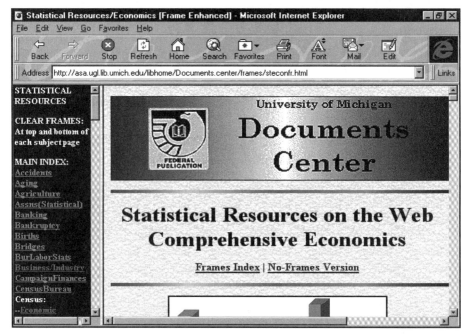

- The University of Michigan Documents Center has compiled this excellent directory and search engine site for statistical and demographic information. Scroll down the home page to see linked titles of available sites along with brief descriptions of their content.

- Scroll down the Main Index to the left of the page to see a complete listing of topic links. Click a link to go directly to information about the topic. Many sites compiled here are presented by state or federal government agencies, though some, such as the Wall Street Research Net, are run by private businesses.

- Available index topics include Industry Construction, City Rankings, Crime, Current Industry Reports, Earnings, Employment, Finance, Fortune 500, HMOs, Labor, Non-Profit Organizations, Producer Prices, Productivity, Social Security, Television Ratings, and

144

Weather. This small sample of the many available topics gives you an idea of the vast amount of data available here.

- Go directly to the bottom of the Documents Center home page to see two other valuable search links. Click the Directory link to go to an alphabetical directory of the site's links. Click the Search link to search the Documents Center Web Site using either the SWISH search engine or the AltaVista search engine.

FedStats

http://www.fedstats.gov

 Use this well-organized, information-packed site to find statistical and demographic information from more than 70 federal government agencies.

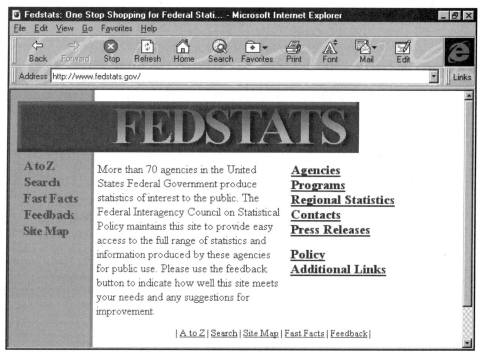

- FedStats is another government Web site that can provide you with a gold mine of useful demographic information. Bet you never thought the government could be so helpful, did you?

- The Federal Interagency Council on Statistical Policy maintains the FedStats site to provide the public with easy access to the mountain of demographic and statistical information the federal government compiles each year.

- Click on the Agencies link to see a listing of the more than 70 government agencies and departments that compile statistics provided on the FedStats site. The agency listing includes links to agency Web sites.

- Click on the Fast Facts link to see a quick synopsis of Fedstats' offerings in a couple of key areas. The Briefing Room here includes links to the latest social and economic indicators. On the Fast Facts page you can also click on links to frequently requested tables, state rankings, and USA statistics in brief direct from the Statistical Abstract of the United States.

- Click on the Programs link to see a description of the various programs for which you can find statistical and demographic information. The narrative text on this page is filled with links that take you directly to corresponding links or Web sites. The Programs page also includes a list of general category links at the top.

- Use the A to Z link to see an alphabetical index of all links to reports and statistics in the FedStats site. If you know what you're looking for, you can also search this vast database by clicking on the Search link and typing in your topic.

Other Sites

CyberAtlas

http://www.cyberatlas.com

- Check this award-winning site for the latest statistics on Internet and World Wide Web usage. Click the links under the Market heading to get a complete demographic breakdown of Internet users. Links include Size, Demographics, Geographics, and Usage Patterns. Be sure to check out the round up of links to Web marketing news highlights featured on the home page.

ZipFind

http://link-usa.com/zipcode/pop.htm

- Use this straightforward site to find the population, population density, and Zip Codes within a given radius of a particular Zip Code. For example, imagine that you want to find how many people live in the 46220 Zip Code. Simply enter the Zip Code in the text box and enter 1 in the radius text box, then click on the Find Population button. You can also look up Zip Codes for cities and towns using this tool.

Research Companies

◆ **BRINT** ◆ **Hoover's Online** ◆ **Dun & Bradstreet**
◆ **Fuld Competitive Intelligence** ◆ **Other Sites**

Search online databases for company information to help you evaluate credit-worthiness of potential customers, research potential clients, and analyze competitors.

BRINT

http://www.brint.com/interest.html

 Excellent search and directory site for finding corporate and competitive information. Hundreds of links to important business Web resources.

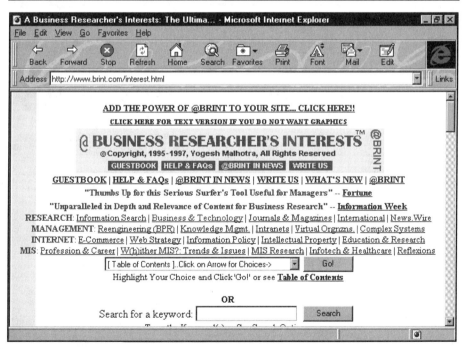

- In many cases, the top Web sites to know are those that can lead you to many other sites. These sites are useful time and again even as your search needs change. The Business Researcher's Interests site (BRINT) is one of the top directory sites for sales research on the Net.

- To find corporate and competitive information, click the Business and Technology link and then click the Company and Industry Information link. From here, you can click on a number of specific Web site links to search for the competitive information you need.

- Company and Industry Information links include more than three dozen top business search sites, such as the Forbes 500 Annual Directory, and Marketing: The Biggest and Best.

- From these Web directories you can find specific company information.

Hoover's Online
http://www.hoovers.com

Search for free company information at the Hoover's Web site. Hoover's online bills itself as "the ultimate source for company information."

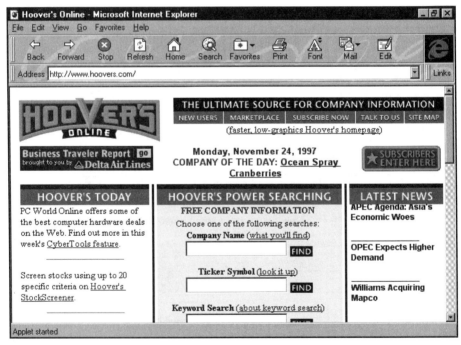

- Hoover's, Inc., is one of the leading publishers of company information, and its Web site is perhaps the best source for low-cost (and free) company data. Hoover's is well known as a publisher of company capsules on more than 11,000 public and private companies around the world.

- Through the Hoover's Web site you can search for a capsule by name or ticker symbol, sort companies based on industry, location, and/or sales. Each company capsule contains basic information you can use to locate, communicate with, and analyze a company.

- To search the Hoover's list of company capsules, go to the home page and enter the company name, a stock ticker symbol, or a keyword. You can also see a business news ticker on the home page.

- Click the Research Stocks link to go to a full-feature investor research page. Click the Boost Your Sales link to see a page that has sales resources such as articles, tips, and links to top sales Web sites.

- Another feature on the Hoover's site you don't want to miss is the Hoover's List of Lists. This page lists links to sites that rank businesses and people in many different categories, including The Biggest & Richest Companies & People, Top Brands, Top Salaries, and Stock Market Performance. Go to: http://hoovers.com/features/whosontop/lists.html.

- Other Hoover's Web sites include IPO Central, Cyberstocks, and Stock Screener. Links to each of these sites can be found on the Hoover's Online site.

Dun & Bradstreet

http://www.dnb.com

 Search the Companies Online database of Dun & Bradstreet, the world's leading distributor of company business and financial information and credit reporting.

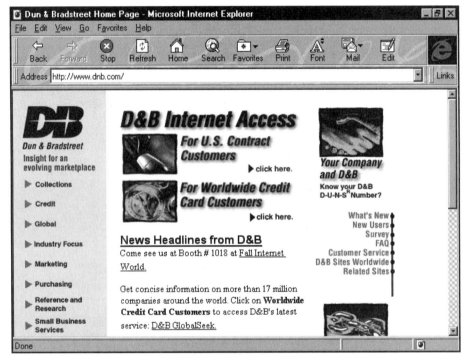

- Log on to the Dun & Bradstreet site primarily to search the Companies Online database, which has been created in partnership with Lycos. You can enter a company name, ticker symbol, and/or URL to begin your free search.

- If you turn up results, you will see a general listing for the company, which includes basic contact information and ownership structure. If you register (free of charge), you can receive information on number of employees, annual sales, holding companies, and other more in-depth data.

- For a $20 fee you can order the Dun & Bradstreet Business Background Report for the company.

- Though Dun & Bradstreet provides excellent, detailed company intelligence, credit reports, and other consulting services, you won't find much more that's free on the Web site. Most links are to marketing or catalog information on Dun & Bradstreet subscriber products.

Fuld Competitive Intelligence

http://www.fuld.com

Fuld & Company corporate site provides numerous links to Web company information resources.

- The Fuld & Company corporate Web site is a great place to start your search for information about competitors and corporate customers. Though this is primarily a corporate marketing site for Fuld's consulting services, you can click the Internet Intelligence Index icon to see a list of links to competitive intelligence sites.

- Links are organized into three general categories: General Business Internet Resources, Industry-Specific Internet Resources, and International Internet Resources.
- General Business Resources links of interest in researching competitors and customers include Company Information, Competitor Intelligence Sites, and Information Services. Click one of these to see links to specific company information sites.
- Industry-Specific Resources links include nearly two dozen industry category links, from Aerospace/Defense to Travel. Click on the industry link you want to search to see links to specific sites. For example, click on the Retailing link to access links to the National Retailing Federation and The World Wide Web Virtual Library for Retailing.

Other Sites

Infoseek Business Channel

http://www.infoseek.com

- Click on the Business channel of this search and directory site to find a wealth of top business links and access to the Hoover's Online company capsules.

Lycos Companies Online

http://www.lycos.com

- Lycos Business Guide includes many valuable business links, Lycos' famous Top 5% sites, and the ability to search the Companies Online database of corporate information, which Lycos runs in partnership with Dun & Bradstreet.

Locate Key People in Your Industry

◆ Four11 ◆ InfoSpace ◆ WorldPages ◆ Other Sites

If you have ever tried to find someone in your industry or locate a potential customer but didn't know where to start, these Web sites are for you. At these sites you can use a number of different search techniques to find the contact information for almost anyone you want to find.

Four11

http://www.four11.com

 Find a business contact or potential customer using the leading Internet "white pages" service. Search by telephone number or by e-mail address.

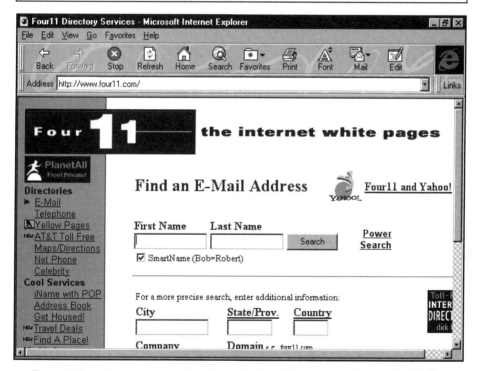

- Four11 has been recognized as the leading Internet people finder site for some time and has recently been acquired by the Yahoo! search and directory site.

- Using Four11, you can enter the name of a person you are looking for along with any additional address information you know about the person and then click Search.

- Click on the Telephone link to search for phone numbers. The Four11 search engine looks for the person in its database of phone directories from across the United States.

- Click on the E-Mail link to search for e-mail addresses. Searching for someone by e-mail address can often prove successful because you can click on the Power Search link to add personal interests and/or previous contact locations to enhance your search.

- The Four11 site also includes a celebrity directory. Click on the Celebrity link to see a directory of celebrity links organized by category, including Actors, Authors/Journalists, Business Leaders, Entertainers, Government, and Sports Stars.

InfoSpace

http://www.infospace.com

 Use reverse e-mail, phone, and address searches at this Web directory site to yield surprisingly effective people search results.

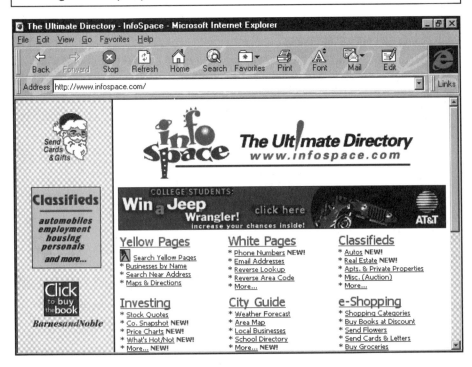

- InfoSpace is a general Web directory site that also happens to have a very good "white pages" service. Click on the White Pages link or any of the White Pages subcategories to begin your search.

- As with Four11, searching for people using InfoSpace is easy. Simply type in the first and last name of the person you're looking for along with any other location information such as a city, state, or address. Click Find to see search results from more than 200 million residential phone numbers and addresses.

- Try using the Reverse Lookup search to find out who belongs to a phone number or e-mail address. Searching with the Reverse E-Mail Lookup can be particularly effective because most business people have e-mail addresses and many e-mail addresses bear some resemblance to the person's name.

- For example, if you were searching for a person named Bob Juliard, you could enter bobjuliard@aol.com or bobj@aol.com to see whether Bob has an AOL account. You can change the access service to search using CompuServe or MSN addresses as well.

- You can also use a reverse address search to find out who lives or works at a particular address. Just enter the address you want and click Find. If you want to see a listing of who lives and works on an entire street, enter just the street name, city name, and state.

- You can also use the InfoSpace "yellow pages" service to search for businesses by location and by name.

WorldPages

http://www.worldpages.com

Search the WorldPages site to find people overseas. You can also search for businesses by location as well as with business and professional headings.

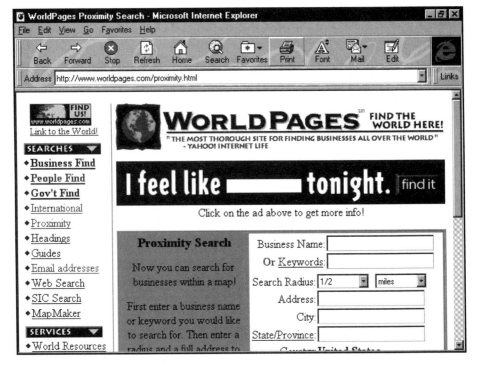

- If you're looking for a business contact overseas, try searching the WorldPages site. Click the International link and then select the country you want to search from the drop-down menu.

- WorldPages also includes a Proximity search for businesses. Click the Proximity link to search for a business by name or by keyword within a particular radius of an address, city, or state. This is a great way to find customer leads within a particular area.

- With the Gov't Find feature, you can search for and locate government agencies by category, city, state, province, or country.

- Click the Headings link to associate your search with a list of common business and professional headings provided by WorldPages. Simply enter your search information in the text boxes and click on any headings you want to add, such as Attorneys and Notary Publics.

- You can also click on the Web Search link to search a database of Web pages for keywords you enter, which can include business and personal names.

Other Sites

WhoWhere?

http://www.whowhere.com

- This top "white pages" search site includes the capability to narrow your search for people by including interests, schools, organizations, location, and/or personal profiles. You can also get free e-mail and post a Web page free of charge at the WhoWhere? site.

Switchboard

http://www.switchboard.com

- Find people or businesses with this directory site. Cool SideClick feature helps you surf the Web "sideways" to find Web sites related to ones you like.

Find Company Contact Information

◆ LocalEyes ◆ WebSitez ◆ BigBook ◆ Other Sites

Search for professional services, suppliers, and other businesses on the Web. Find potential customers and clients with these leading directories and search engines.

LocalEyes

http://www8.localeyes.com

 Find business and professional services in dozens of metro areas across the country with this "yellow pages" type directory and search tool.

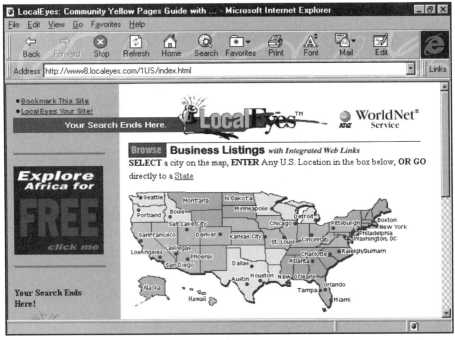

- Use the LocalEyes search site to find businesses and potential clients in your community or any area across the country. From the LocalEyes home page you can enter a search phrase such as *Accountants in Cleveland*, then click Search. From the search results, you can then click a link and go directly to the firm or site you want.

- You can also enter a city, state, or Zip Code to go to a LocalEyes metro page. From a metro page you can select a directory category such as Business & Professional or Money & Finance to narrow your search.

- Enter a business name or topic in the search engine at a metro page to search LocalEyes listings only in that area. Include a Zip Code in the search criteria to narrow the search further.

- LocalEyes also includes links to other metro area sites including shopping mall listings, weather, TV listings, and recommended Great Sites.

WebSitez

http://www.websitez.com

 Did you forget a Web address or the name of a company you wanted to contact? Find Web sites and company names using this powerful database of more than 1 million Web addresses.

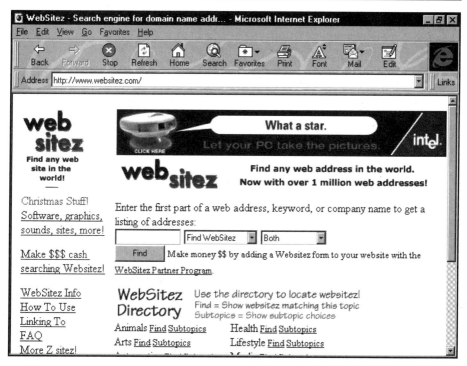

- If you want to contact a prospective client and all you know is the company name or even part of the company name, try a search at the WebSitez home page. By using WebSitez, you can avoid trying to guess a company's URL and avoid those annoying "404 Server Not Found" errors.

- Because more Web sites are added to the Internet each day and because many company names are similar, Web addresses often do not seem logical. The URLs may be a shortened version of the company name, they may include hyphens, or they may by necessity or by choice use some word altogether different from the company name.

- To search for a site, enter what you know about the company you want to find, choose whether you want to find Web sites, files, or FTP sites, and then choose whether you want to see Web site names, company names, or both displayed in the search results. WebSitez searches a database of more than 1 million Web addresses, and its fast servers return results quickly.

- Search results display categories that match or nearly match your search criteria. The number of site or name matches within each category also appears. Click on a category to see links to Web sites and/or company names. Company information can also be displayed.

- WebSitez comes in handy if you have forgotten a Web address or if you simply want to enter keywords to find sites that match your interest. You can also use a WebSitez search to identify unused addresses for your own use. WebSitez search results include check marks showing which sites were active as of the last WebSitez test of the site.

BigBook

http://www.bigbook.com

 Find any business or professional service quickly. Listings include exact location shown on a map as well as driving directions.

- BigBook is one of the leading online "yellow pages" sites, offering a number of added value services that can help you find the business or professional service firm you're looking for quickly and easily.

- You can search for a business or service several ways with BigBook. You can enter either a business (e.g. Hilton) or a category (e.g. Hotels) in the search text box and then enter a city and/or state to search. You can also click on links to available search categories.

- If you want to find nearby businesses, you can use either the Search Nearby tool or the Detailed Search tool. With Search Nearby, you can specify a business or category and then a distance from a specific address. For example, I found that there are 30 lawyers and 8 pizza parlors within a 1-mile radius of my home address.

- With Detailed Search, you specify a business or category and then a specific street name, area code, city, state, or Zip Code. The search results will list all of the businesses you asked for in that specific location.

- After you receive the search results page, which includes addresses and phone numbers, you can click on a specific listing to see a map showing the business location. Click on the Driving Directions icon and enter your location to find out how to get there.

- BigBook also includes links to sales leads, mailing lists, business profiles, and credit ratings provided by American Business Information.

Other Sites

BigYellow

http://www.bigyellow.com

- This top-flight "yellow pages" directory includes more than 16 million U.S. business listings.

NetPartners Company Search

http://www.netpart.com/resource/search.html

- Use this search engine to find a company's Web or FTP site. You can enter a company name, a partial company name, or a company domain name (such as company.com). The engine sometimes takes a while to grind through the InterNIC database of U.S. companies, but it usually finds its mark.

Toll-Free Internet Directory

http://www.tollfree.att.net/dir800/

- Visit this site for a searchable directory of toll-free phone numbers.

Improve Sales Techniques

◆ SalesDoctors Magazine ◆ Trade Show News Network ◆ Other Sites

Constant effort is required to improve your sales results. Use these sites to learn new selling techniques that can make you more successful. Each of the sites listed here offers practical, how-to information and access to tools that can help you close sales.

SalesDoctors Magazine

http://www.salesdoctors.com

 This is the ultimate selling resource on the Web. Turn here for answers, advice, how-to articles, and links to the best sales tools available online.

- SalesDoctors Magazine has been named the number one sales Web site by Entrepreneur Magazine, and with good reason. This site is the most complete resource for selling professionals available online.

- The SalesDoctors Web site is just as filled with useful tips, selling strategies, and sales resources as the paper version of the magazine. The online magazine even has a couple of advantages over its hardcopy counterpart. You can click on links to related sites, browse the magazine archives, and check current content for the information you need.

- From the SalesDoctors home page, click on the Current Issue link to read 8-10 new articles on sales, service, management, and marketing. A new issue appears with updated content every Monday morning. Click on the Prior Issues link to review the preceding 20 weeks of the magazine.

- Click on the SalesDoctors Archives link to search more than 600 articles from leading sales experts. You can search the archives by department or by the name of featured sales experts.

- The Special Features column of the home page contains special links to departments such as House Calls (an online sales coaching class), First Aid Clinic (hundreds of tips from SalesDoctors readers), Laser Surgery (quick cures for sales ailments), and Featured Sales Experts.

- Click on the Managers and Trainers link to see ideas for using SalesDoctors articles and features in your company's training. The Mental Health link takes you to motivational articles for dealing with bumps along the road to success.

- The More Resources link contains links to hundreds of tools and services to make your life as a selling professional easier. And don't pass up the SalesDoctors Free link, which offers a directory of links to free sites, business tools, software, and services available on the Web.

Trade Show News Network

http://www.tsnn.com

 Get practical advice on improving trade show sales techniques. Find out where trade shows will be held and make arrangements to travel to the shows.

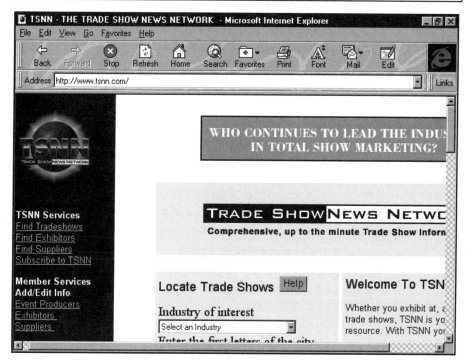

- Trade shows can provide a focused, high visibility means of connecting with your customers. However, if you lack effective exhibit planning and booth selling techniques, your trade show presence can do more harm than good.

- Trade shows can also be a rather expensive way to reach your audience. Before you spend a big chunk of your marketing budget on a show, use the Trade Show News Network (TSNN) to help you plan your trade show selling strategy.

- The TSNN site provides outstanding practical information whether you plan, present, or attend trade shows. Check the News and Resources links to find out industry news, events, and opportunities in the world of exhibitors. The Trade Show News link takes you to a Top Ten News Stories link, news from around the industry, and a link to a weekly newsletter update.

- Home page news stories feature stories such as "The Psychology of Handshakes," exhibitor tips, and an Ask the Expert column that provides practical how-to information to improve your performance in the booth.
- Click on the Find Tradeshows link to search for the type, time, and location of a trade show you want to attend, or simply use the search engine text boxes available on the home page for locating a trade show.
- Click the Find Exhibitors link to search for companies participating in the trade show industry. Click Find Suppliers to locate exhibit supply companies. Exhibitors and suppliers in the index are members of TSNN, and you must join if you wish to be included in the database.

Other Sites

The Selling Arena
http://www.psahome.com

- The Selling Arena site is designed to help sales professionals maximize their performance through news articles, expert tips and advice, as well as sales conference and chat sites. Links to travel, media, and research Web sites provide useful selling resources.

Entrepreneurial Edge Online
http://www.edgeonline.com

- Selling is all about being in business for yourself, and this online magazine site offers sage advice and informative features for the enterprising sales rep. Be sure to check the Business Resources and Business Builders links.

RepLink
http://www.replink.com

- Use RepLink to find either a sales representative for your products or a product to represent. This site is not a job posting board. Rather, it is a matchmaking service for manufacturers, sales agents, representatives, wholesalers, and distributors. Manufacturers can grow their territory quickly with this service. Sales agents can easily add new products to their list.

Trade Show Central
http://www.tscentral.com

- This free Web site provides information on more than 30,000 trade shows, conferences, and seminars. Whether you wish to attend or exhibit, this search engine and directory will help you find shows in your industry. You can access show and registration information directly from the Trade Show Central site.

Market Your Product on the Web

◆ **Web Marketing Info Center** ◆ **The Home Page Maker**
◆ **CIO WebBusiness** ◆ **LinkExchange** ◆ **Other Sites**

Leverage the marketing power of the Web by consulting these sites. Free instruction and advice as well as professional fee-based services are available to help you set up shop online successfully.

Web Marketing Info Center

http://www.wilsonweb.com/webmarket/

 The place to go for the best collection of Web marketing and site building resources and information.

■ Getting started is often the hardest part of any undertaking, and the same holds true for marketing your products or services on the Web. Unless your company is large enough to hire an outside firm to launch and manage your site, the technical aspects of creating a corporate home page can be daunting.

- In addition, once you get past the initial task of getting a site up and running, you're faced with the challenge of getting the site noticed and generating traffic and sales.

- The Web Marketing Info Center is perhaps the top resource available on the Web for meeting these challenges head on. The people at Wilson Internet Services, a Web page design and consulting firm, have compiled a comprehensive collection of articles and resources to help you find the information you need to market your company on the Web.

- The Web Marketing Info Center page is thoughtfully organized to help you find the right resources. A link directory appears at the right of the page, including such topics as Banner Advertising Models, Branding on the Web, and Demographics of the Web. Click one of these topic links to browse a page devoted to the subject, complete with many links to associated articles.

- Another series of topical links is displayed at the left of the Marketing Info Center home page. There are dozens of category links here that take you to dozens of articles on each subject.

- If you're just starting out and the array of choices available on the Web Marketing Info Center page seems a little overwhelming, scroll down the page to find four links to good introductory articles.

- Another bonus of checking out this Web page: If you like what you see here, you can contact Wilson Internet Services to have them start helping you build your site.

The Home Page Maker

http://www.wizard.com/~fifi/pagemake.html

Create a quick and easy Web page for yourself or for your business using this site. Simple instructions walk you through entering information and choosing page design elements.

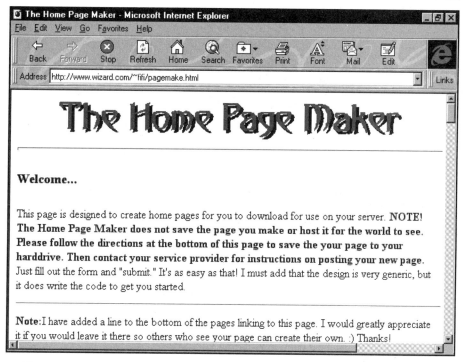

- If you want to get started right away with a quick home page for your business or yourself and you don't have the time to invest in learning how to program HTML, try using The Home Page Maker.

- This handy site, prepared by an individual and available free of charge, walks you through a simple input form for entering your personal and/or business information. Then you enter a few favorite places on the Web that can be included as links on your page.

- After you enter your basic information into the form, you can select colors for the various text and graphical elements of your page. Remember to keep the color scheme simple and avoid using too many fonts and graphical elements.

- Finally, you can enter a famous quote or some words of wisdom you want to appear on your new Web page. Perhaps a company slogan or marketing phrase can go here.

- Click the Make My Page button to create the code for your Web page. Note that you must save the page to your computer system yourself. The Home Page Maker site does not automatically do that for you.

CIO WebBusiness

http://webbusiness.cio.com

 Satisfy the gearhead in you by checking out the latest in Webmaster shoptalk at CIO WebBusiness.

- If you're a professional Webmaster or if you just want to read about what the pros do, check out the CIO WebBusiness page for high-powered information on designing and maintaining a corporate Web site.

- CIO Magazine is a trade publication for information technology professionals. The complete online version of the magazine can be accessed by clicking on the CIO Magazine link at the left of the page.

- Click on one of the WebBusiness Research Center links to learn about the challenges of life as a professional Webmaster. Each page is loaded with links to in-depth and highly technical information, from articles to features to white papers.

- Click on links to other resources such as Web Professional Wanted, Webmaster Archives, and Web Events. Feature articles from the current issue of CIO Magazine are also available.

LinkExchange

http://www.linkexchange.com

 This free service puts you in touch with more than 200,000 Web sites with which you can exchange Web links and advertising space to improve your exposure on the Web.

- Visit this top site for generating hits at your company Web site. LinkExchange puts its members in contact with each other so that they can exchange advertising and links on each other's Web sites.

- The idea is simple, but powerful. The more ads exchanged, the greater the likelihood of someone clicking on your site. What's more, you're generating additional exposure by essentially giving away something that doesn't cost you anything but space on your page.

- Webmaster membership at LinkExchange is free upon registration. Membership allows you to exchange ads with other members, purchase targeted Web advertising packages, and search the database of more than 200,000 members.
- Member or not, you can click on the Resources for Web site owners link to get information for improving the design and traffic flow at your Web site.

Other Sites

Website Promoter's Resource Center

http://www.wprc.com/

- This top site for improving traffic to your Web site includes resources and information on banner advertising, URL submission, targeted e-mail, and press releases.

Relevant Knowledge

http://www.relevantknowledge.com

- Relevant Knowledge will help you track and measure your Web site's audience. How many people are you reaching online? Who are they, and will they buy anything from you? Relevant Knowledge can tell you the answers—but for a fee.

Mouse Tracks

http://nsns.com/MouseTracks/

- Mouse Tracks is a good site to check for periodic updates on trends and developments in Web marketing. Includes links to conferences, articles, and commentary online.

Develop Direct Marketing Online

◆ Eagle Direct Marketing ◆ American List Counsel
◆ PostMaster Direct Response ◆ Other Sites

The ability to search databases and send messages online makes the Web a perfect place to develop direct marketing campaigns. Find sites that have searchable mailing lists or direct e-mail services that can help you cut mailing costs and hit your target market.

Eagle Direct Marketing

http://eagle.multiactive.com/

 Eagle provides a sample search that shows the power of narrowing direct marketing lists online.

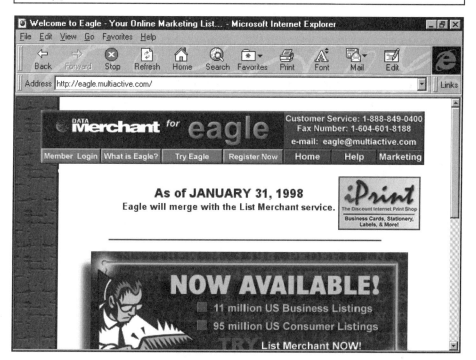

- The Eagle Direct Marketing site provides a good example of the type of direct marketing services available on the Web.

- The power of database marketing on the Web is the speed with which you can access a variety of list providers and their lists. In many cases you can search direct marketing lists online before you buy, thus eliminating stale and inappropriate listings and lowering your cost.

- Click on the Try Eagle link to conduct a sample search of one of Eagle's databases according to criteria you enter. This demonstration will give you an idea of the powerful service online list providers can offer.

- At the Eagle site, you can register to search and narrow its lists for free. Then, when you have a list that meets your needs, you pay only for the listings you have selected.

American List Counsel

http://www.amlist.com

 Find searchable lists and great information about direct mail marketing.

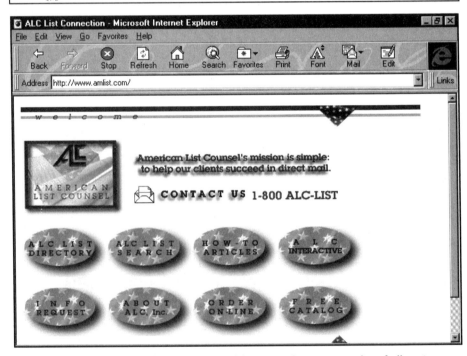

- The American List Counsel provides another example of direct marketing services available online.

174

- Click on the ALC List Directory icon to see a directory of links to available lists that you can browse by SIC (Standard Industrial Classification) code or by category. Click on the ALC List Search to perform a keyword search of the lists. Search results show ALC lists that match your entry.

- Click on the How-To Articles to see a listing of links to some very good information and tips about direct mail marketing.

PostMaster Direct Response

http://www.postmasterdirect.com/welcome.mhtml

 Hit your target market online with direct e-mail marketing.

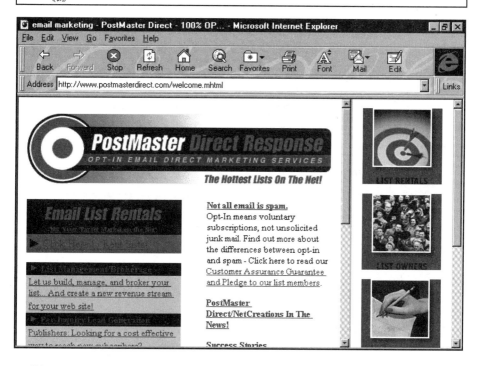

- Direct marketing works just as well using e-mail as with paper. Just be careful to avoid what's commonly called *spamming* on the Web. Spamming is the unsolicited delivery of e-mail sales messages to a wide target audience.

- Spamming tends to generate a rather vehement backlash from some members of the Internet community, and it certainly is less effective than a well-targeted electronic mailing.
- Check sites such as PostMaster Direct Response to find what are called "opt-in" lists—lists of people who voluntarily request information about a particular topic. Messages sent from these lists are received in a kinder light in the online world and tend to receive a better response rate.
- PostMaster Direct Response services include per-inquiry lead generation, in which you pay for leads generated in response to a free sample or trial offer, and list management and brokerage.

Other Sites

Database America

http://www.databaseamerica.com/html/index.htm

- This online sales lead and direct marketing development site provides numerous services, including list services, computer services, and interactive media. Available lists include 11,000,000 businesses and 95 million households in target marketing databases.

targ*it e-mail

http://www.targ-it.com/index.htm

- Purchase targeted e-mail lists for use in your online direct marketing campaigns. targ*it e-mail provides lists of more than 40,000 Webmasters, more than 50,000 online magazine subscribers, 75,000 business professionals, and 500,000 catalog shoppers. All lists on the targ*it site are opt-in lists, developed using information from people who have indicated a desire to be receive mail about a particular topic.

Sell to the Government

◆ **CBDNet** ◆ **FedWorld Information Network** ◆ **Thomas** ◆ **Other Sites**

The federal government can be the source of millions of dollars of potential sales, but you often need to cut through a maze of bureaus, agencies, departments, and red tape to close a government sale. These Web sites can help you cut through the bureaucracy and locate what you need to win government contracts, research laws or regulations, register your intellectual property, or keep up to date with Congressional activities that may affect your industry.

CBDNet

http://cbdnet.access.gpo.gov/index.html

 Find government contract opportunities by searching the Department of Commerce database of procurement notices.

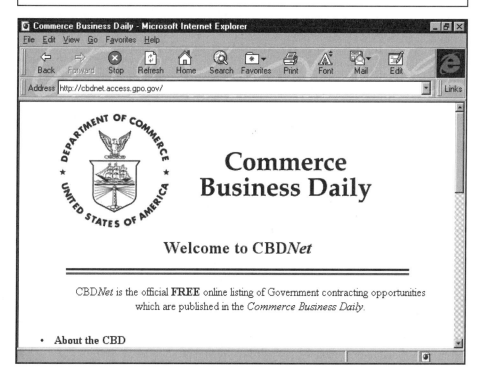

- Find government procurement opportunities online at the Commerce Business Daily (CBD) page, CBDNet, part of the Department of Commerce Web site. CBD regularly updates a database of government procurements, contract awards, and sales of government property.

- Search CBD to find opportunities for doing business with the federal government. All proposed government contracts and procurements over $25,000 are required by law to be listed in the CBD database.

- You can conduct either a simple search or a fielded search of the CBD database. For a simple search, you only need to enter a keyword or keywords. Use the fielded search if you want to look up specific segments of the CBD database or if you want to use operators to narrow your search criteria.

- The CBD database contains all active notices of government contract requisitions. The database is updated continuously with new requisitions. Notices of requisition remain in the active database for 15 days, after which they are moved permanently to an archive database. You can also include the archive database in your searches.

- After you receive search results, you can click links to see the actual procurement notice text.

FedWorld Information Network

http://www.fedworld.gov

 Search more than 300,000 government information products and get the latest government job postings.

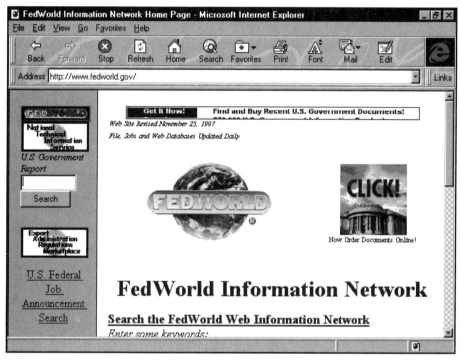

- Start your search for government information with FedWorld, a directory site administered by the National Technical Information Service of the U.S. Department of Commerce. FedWorld is the best place to look for information produced by or about the U.S. federal government, including regulations, articles, job opportunities, and searchable databases.

- Click on the U.S. Business Advisor link to access the government's chief source of information for business. Here you can get answers to common questions that businesses ask the government, how-to guides and tools, a search engine for regulations and information, and a browse page containing government sites organized by topic.

- Click on the U.S. Federal Job Announcement Search link to search the government's USAJOBS Web site and FJOB bulletin board system created and administered by the Office of Personnel Management. This search is the quickest way to cut through the government bureaucratic maze and find specific federal job listings.

- From the FedWorld home page you can also click drop-down lists of government agencies, services, and Web sites to search, including general information services, FedWorld-hosted Web sites, and further information about FedWorld.

Thomas

http://thomas.loc.gov

 Follow the current activities of the U.S. Congress and research past federal legislation. This site includes complete directories of the Senate and the House of Representatives.

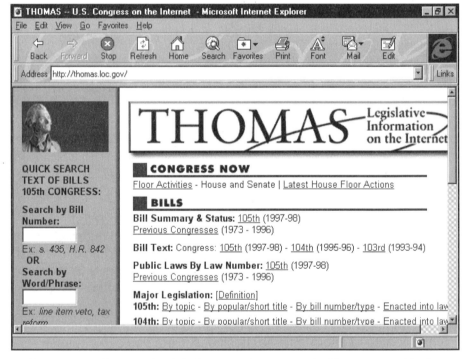

- Keep up to date on legislative developments in Congress with the Thomas Web site. A service of the Library of Congress named after Thomas Jefferson, this site is the ultimate source for information about the activities of both the U.S. Senate and the House of Representatives.

180

- Use the Thomas search engine to search several databases, including the current week's floor activities of Congress as well as text, summaries, and/or activities surrounding current and historical bills (historical meaning prior to 1973). Other searchable databases include Congressional Record text and index, Congressional committee reports and home pages, and historical documents (important documents from the founding of the United States).

- You can also find articles describing the legislative process, and links to Internet resources for government entities such as the House and Senate Web pages, Library of Congress, General Accounting Office, and Congressional Budget Office.

- The Thomas home page has been recently redesigned for quick-click access to the most-used sites and search engines. Click links in the Congress Now section of the page to see summaries of bills currently on the floor. Click links in the Bills section to see summaries of bills organized by session of Congress. Other home page sections include Congressional Record, Committee Information, The Legislative Process, and Historical Documents.

- You can also click Thomas home page links to directories for members of the Senate and the House of Representatives.

Other Sites

Federal Web Locator

http://www.law.vill.edu/Fed-Agency/fedwebloc.html

- This clearinghouse directory of federal information and resources is provided by the Villanova Center for Information Law and Policy. It includes a well-organized index of links to all government agency and department Web sites.

FedLaw

http://www.legal.gsa.gov/

- This is the complete hyperlinked text of federal laws and regulations. You can search the complete text of the U.S. Code by title and section.

Government Information Exchange

http://www.info.gov/Info/html/phone_directories.htm

- This site indexes links for phone directories of all branches, departments, and agencies of the federal government. The Federal Yellow Pages at this site includes links to all government departments, agencies, and services.

Sell Your Products in Other Countries

◆ **International Business Resources on the WWW**
◆ **NAFTAnet** ◆ **Other Sites**

Expand your markets by exporting your product to other countries with the help of these sites. The two featured sites provide excellent search and directory starting points for finding international trade resources online. Other sites help you make contacts with import/export partners overseas.

International Business Resources on the WWW

http://ciber.bus.msu.edu/busres.htm

 Start your quest for information about expanding your global sales presence here. This is the top search and directory site for research on international trade.

- The best place to start your search for help in international sales is the International Business Resources on the WWW site, produced by Michigan State University's Center for International Business Education and Research. This is a superb directory site for finding online information and business links about international trade. The site has received a number of awards from online and computer magazines.

- Like most good directory sites, you can either search or browse to find what you want. Type keywords in the search textbox and click on the Search Now! button.

- Scroll down the home page to browse the index of about twenty category links. Click on a link that interests you to see a page of Web site links for that topic along with a brief description of each site.

NAFTAnet

http://www.nafta.net

 Find opportunities for expanding your markets in Mexico and Canada at this excellent directory site produced with the bottom line in mind.

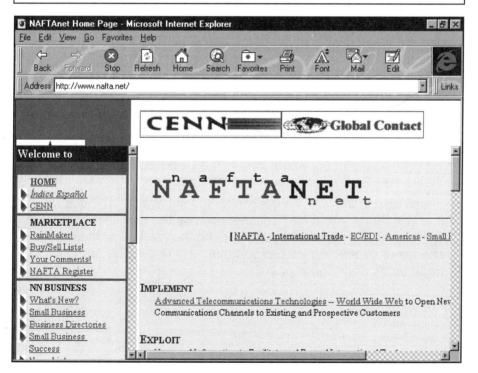

- How can you take advantage of trade opportunities that may be available due to NAFTA, the North American Free Trade Agreement? One of the best ways to find out is to consult NAFTAnet, a directory site listing links to dozens of sites pertaining to trade with our neighbors to the north and south.

- Links on the main section of the home page are organized according to ways you can take advantage of NAFTA to grow your business.

- Click the Advanced Telecommunications Technologies—World Wide Web link to learn more about using the Web to reach NAFTA trading partners.

- Click the Exploit links for pertinent news articles, legal information, and other market and industry updates.

- Click the Reduce links to learn more about clearance, security, commercial technology, and ways to save time and money while doing business on the Internet.

- Go to the Target links to gather statistics about the impact of NAFTA trade and learn which industries are benefiting from NAFTA.

- Use the Welcome To menu at the left of the home page to click on bottom-line oriented topics such as Rainmaker, Buy/Sell Lists, Small Business Success, and $Market, the site's Marketplace section.

- Click on the NAFTA link near the top of the home page to see the entire text of the agreement as well as useful links to the NAFTA Implementation Resource Guide and the NAFTA Impact Update. You can also find out about GATT, the General Agreement on Tariffs and Trade, in this section of the directory.

- Check also in the NAFTA section for the list of Top 40 Industries that Will Benefit from NAFTA, prepared by the U.S. Department of Commerce. If your industry appears on the list, you stand a good chance of expanding your export business due to the reduction of trade tariffs and regulations.

Other Sites

BusinessEurope

http://www.businesseurope.com

- Search this site by country to find American Embassy reports, trade fair information, a trade bulletin board, and articles about trade in Europe.

International Business List

http://www.earthone.com/internat.html

- This Web site provides a place where business people can meet to make contacts and find new trading partners. It also features a message center for those seeking jobs, consultants, or other international business services.

World Access Network Direct

http://www.wand.com

- This site matches buyers and sellers in the global import/export trade. Search the database of postings by SIC or Harmonized Code, or by manufacturer. After you locate a match for your needs, WAND supplies contact information.

The CIA World Factbook

http://www.odci.gov/cia/publications/nsolo/wfb-all.htm

- Usually not known for giving away its information, the CIA supplies a full helping of its "intelligence" at this Web site. Search here for all kinds of statistical and cultural information about countries, regions, and populations around the world. Information is indexed alphabetically for easy searching. Be sure to view this site's great maps.

Plan and Book Travel Online

◆ **Microsoft Expedia** ◆ **Bed and Breakfast Inns Online** ◆ **Zagat Survey**
◆ **MapQuest** ◆ **Other Sites**

Use the Web to make your next business trip more enjoyable and more
cost effective. There are dozens of excellent travel-related sites that can
help you plan your trip, search for travel bargains, and book tickets online.
These top travel Web sites provide a good sample of the kinds of
resources available online to help you.

Microsoft Expedia

http://expedia.msn.com/daily/home/default.hts

 Use this award-winning Web site to explore destinations,
plan your trip itinerary, and book travel online.

- Microsoft Expedia is the award-winning travel Web site produced by
  the software giant as part of its Microsoft Network online service. The
  site has been named one of the top 100 Web sites by PC Magazine, a
  Yahoo! Internet Life Five-Star Award-winner (one of only 12 per year),
  and a Top Ten PCWeek E-Commerce winner.

- The site receives these awards with good reason. First, it's a pleasure to look at, with a rich attractive Web page design. It's also full of information about where to go and what to do. Click on the Resources link to browse the World Guide, a complete online travel guidebook, check weather, and use a currency converter.

- Click on Magazine to read articles about travel destinations, news briefs and bargain updates, as well as featured columnists and ideas about fresh approaches to travel that can make your trip more enjoyable.

- The beauty of most travel Web sites is the capability to plan and book travel online. Expedia offers a number of powerful search and booking tools at its Travel Agent link. Click here to find low airfares and book airline tickets. You can also search for available hotel rooms at your destination and reserve rooms. If you need a rental car, you can find and reserve one here too.

Bed and Breakfast Inns Online
http://www.bbonline.com

 Find a distinctive place to stay on your next business trip that will save you money and allow you to enjoy your destination more.

- One way to make business travel more enjoyable is to avoid cookie-cutter chain hotels and stay at a small inn that lets you experience a little more of what life is like in the town you're visiting.

- Bed & Breakfasts Online provides a guide to more than 2,000 bed and breakfasts and country inns across the United States. You may be surprised by how many fine inns are available at very reasonable rates, in many cases less expensive than staying at a chain hotel.

- You will also find that many inns and bed and breakfasts are located in major cities, close to where you do business. Click on the Locate a B&B link at the Bed & Breakfasts Online home page to begin your search.

- You can search the site's database by location in the United States, Canada, Mexico, and the Caribbean. U.S. listings are organized by region and then by state.

- You can also search several directories of inns with distinctive features, such as being on the ocean or in the mountains, being on the National Register of Historic Places, or those offering special package deals. The site also includes links to state innkeeper association Web sites.

Zagat Survey

http://www.pathfinder.com/travel/Zagat

 Find the right restaurant for your next business meal by consulting the Zagat Survey online. Complete directory of survey listings and reviews for 40 major U.S. cities.

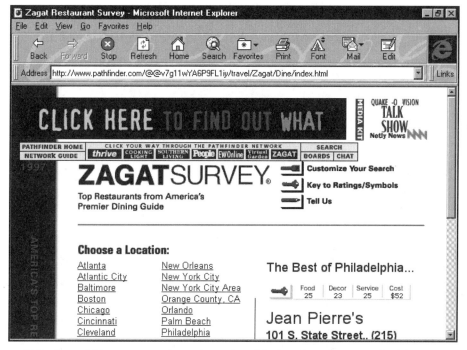

- What could be worse than dropping big bucks on a meal with a client (or prospective client) and having the meal turn out to be less than impressive, even downright awful? Consulting the Zagat Survey Web site beforehand is a great way to avoid a bad business meal on the road.

- The Zagat Survey is widely recognized as the leading guide to fine dining across the country. Click on a city link to view an alphabetical index of restaurant listings for the city. You can also search the listings directory by cuisine, by food ranking, or by best deals.

- If you already know the name of the restaurant you want to find, just type it into the search engine text box and click on Find It!

- Each link to a restaurant listing has a one- or two-word description of the type of restaurant (such as French, vegetarian, or Tex-Mex) to help you sift among the many possibilities. Click on a restaurant link to read the Zagat review. The survey rates each restaurant by food, decor, and service on a scale of 0 to 30. The cost of an average dinner plus drink and tip is also listed.

MapQuest

http://www.mapquest.com

 Don't get lost on your way to an important appointment. Check the MapQuest site for door-to-door driving directions and interactive maps of any location in the continental U.S.

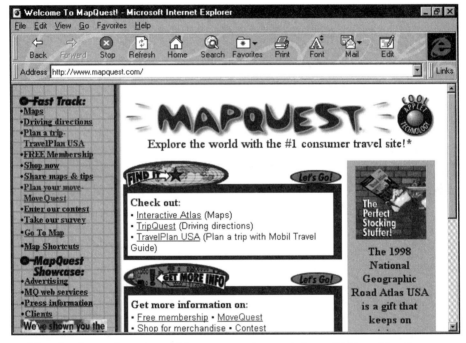

- Need to know how to get to your next appointment? Head for the MapQuest Web site to find out the best way to get to your destination.

- Click on the TripQuest link to find driving directions from point A to point B. Simply type the address of your starting point in the TripQuest form, then type in the address of your destination.

- You can choose several mapping options for your directions, including city-to-city or door-to-door with an overview map, turn-by-turn maps with text, or text only. Door-to-door directions are provided for 29 major metro areas. City-to-city routing is provided from any town or city to any other town or city within the continental U.S. and some parts of Mexico and Canada.

- If you want to find your own way, click on the Interactive Atlas link on the home page. At the Interactive Atlas page, you can enter a point of interest or an address to view a map of that location. You can zoom in or zoom out to view more or less area and detail on the maps.
- Click on the TravelPlan USA link at the MapQuest home page to plan your next trip using the Mobil Travel Guide.

Other Sites

The Trip
http://www.thetrip.com

- Among the many travel Web sites available, The Trip stands out because of its attention to the needs of business travelers. The Trip has a no-nonsense, no-hassle approach to planning and booking enjoyable travel. Be sure to check out the Airport Strategies link for information about making your flight connections.

FareFinder

http://www.reservations.com/Farefinder/

- To find the lowest airfares available today, check Preview Travel's Farefinder service. A ticker of lowest fares between various cities nationwide appears at the top of the page. Enter your departure city and destination to find the lowest fares currently available.

Subway Navigator

http://metro.jussieu.fr:10001/bin/cities/english

- Find the route from one destination to another using this routing service for subway or rail systems in major cities around the world.

Travlang Foreign Languages for Travelers

http://www.travlang.com

- Extensive directory of language resources for study and translation of languages from around the world. Includes links to Web resources for even the most obscure languages. The site also offers international travel services such as overseas hotel listings, air reservations, and currency exchange information.

Check Weather Reports for Sales Travel

◆ Intellicast ◆ Weather.com ◆ Other Sites

Get up-to-the-minute weather forecasts for any location across the country or around the world to help you plan for sales call travel.

Intellicast

http://www.intellicast.com

 The most complete weather site on the Web, including four-day forecasts, national weather maps and radar loops, as well as complete travel forecasts, up-and-running almanacs, and long-range forecasts for all regions of the country.

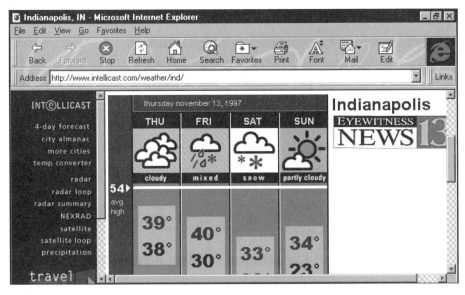

- What will the weather hold for you today? Will driving conditions be hazardous? Should you expect weather-related flight delays? What should you pack if you're flying from Chicago to Los Angeles, or vice versa? Intellicast gives you all the answers to these questions at one very informative Web site.

- Get the local four-day forecast for cities around the world. You can also check local radar loops that update every 15 minutes to see where stormy weather is heading.

Check Weather Reports for Sales Travel

- Use the Travel Weather feature to check national maps for various types of inclement weather, including RainCast, SnowCast, FogCast, WindCast, and ThunderstormCast.

- Use FlightCast to find the current city forecast, flight status, and estimated departure and arrival times for flights currently in progress. Simply enter the departure and arrival cities along with either the departure or arrival time to find the information you need. You can also enter the airline name and flight number.

- Intellicast has extensive background information on weather phenomena and long-term forecasting. Other useful features include an influenza map and the Dr. Dewpoint question and answer service, as well as ski, tropical, and national park reports. Intellicast has all the information you'll need, whether you're flying across country or just deciding whether to bring along an umbrella to the office.

Weather.com
http://www.weather.com

 Not quite as complete as Intellicast, but all the basic weather information you need is here, including local five-day forecasts and flight delay updates.

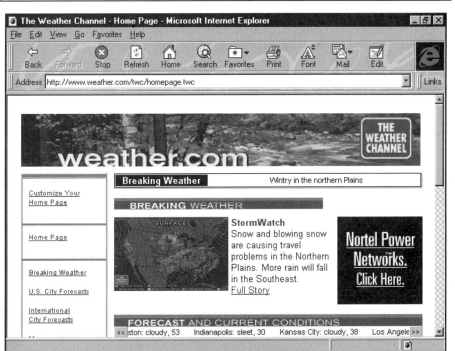

- The Weather Channel Web site offers most of the same features you can find on the Intellicast site, though the site appears to be "under construction" in many places. Enter a city or state name from the home page and see a five-day forecast. The Forecast and Current Conditions ticker is a convenient way to get the latest conditions at a glance.

- Go to the Travel Conditions page to see flight delays for thirty-five major airports across the country. You can also enter specific flight information to see estimated arrival flight times.

- You can customize your Weather Channel home page to include forecasts for up to five cities (from more than 1,600 worldwide), include five maps, travel and trivia information. If you want to change the page in the future, you can modify it or revert back to the standard Weather Channel home page.

- The Breaking Weather feature includes information on current weather happenings, tropical storm updates, and severe weather alerts, as well as background information about weather phenomena such as El Niño and a Storm Encyclopedia with interesting accounts of the greatest storms in history. Another highlight is Weather Channel access to Britannica Online weather entries.

- The Project Safeside feature is a collaborated effort of the American Red Cross and the Weather Channel to provide safety and preparedness education to American families. In addition to providing critical information about the five most deadly weather-related events, Project Safeside also has links to current disaster relief efforts.

- Other helpful features include a Health and Allergies section with current maps of conditions for allergy sufferers, boat and beach forecasts, and gardening tips. Overall, the Weather Channel page has a lot to offer to business and pleasure travelers alike.

Other Sites

- Almost every major Web directory and news site includes some form of weather update and forecast. If you're on your way to finding other information via the Web, you can also check these sites for weather conditions, though the sites may not provide all the information you can find at exclusively weather-oriented sites.

- Following are a few of the more popular news and directory sites that include weather information:

Excite
http://www.my.excite.com/weather/

Yahoo
http://weather.yahoo.com/

Lycos
http://weather.lycos.com/default.asp

New York Times
http://www.nytimes.com/weather/

CNN Interactive
http://www.cnn.com/WEATHER/

Check Traffic Conditions

◆ Yahoo! Traffic ◆ AccuTraffic

Check traffic conditions before you hit the road for sales travel or even a daily commute. These sites can alert you to potential delays in major metropolitan areas across the country.

Yahoo! Traffic

http://www.yahoo.com

 Use the popular search and directory site to find real-time traffic information for a dozen major metropolitan areas across the country.

- Yahoo! is one of the top sites on the Web to search for any kind of information you care to find. Tucked away among all of the great information at Yahoo! you can check real-time traffic conditions for a dozen major metro areas across the U.S., including New York, Chicago, Los Angeles, and San Francisco.

- From the Yahoo! home page, click one of the Yahoo! Metro sites at the bottom of the page and then click the Traffic link from the Metro page for the city you choose. Traffic updates for each city are maintained by different traffic Web sites, so features will vary from city to city. However, most traffic sites include alerts about traffic delays as well as real-time maps and/or listings of traffic flow on major freeways.

- For example, at the Chicago traffic site provided by Maxwell Technologies, you can click a link for a region of the metropolitan area, then choose either a clickable map showing real-time freeway speeds or a table with real-time freeway speeds clocked at various interchanges.

- You can also click on the Get Local link from the Yahoo! home page and then enter a Zip Code or click on a state link to find Yahoo! sites for other cities. If there is a traffic Web site available for a particular city, you are likely to find a link to the site from the Yahoo! city page.

AccuTraffic

http://www.accutraffic.com

 As with many freeways, this site is under construction, but it shows potential in its ambition to be a nationwide collection of metro traffic sites. Only one or two cities are currently available.

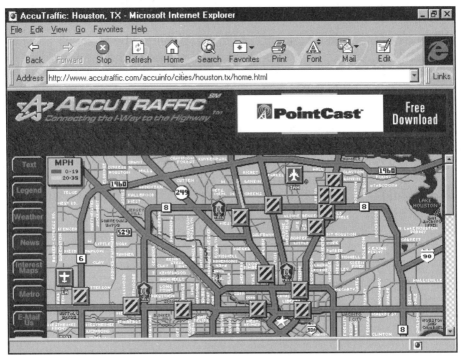

- AccuTraffic seeks to build a collection of dozens of metro area traffic report sites, but most of these sites are not active yet. When they do go live, however, AccuTraffic plans to be the top one-stop site for checking metro traffic conditions.

- The maps and graphics on display at the Houston page, one of the few AccuTraffic sites currently up and running, are clear and easy to use. Slow-down areas on freeways are color coded by speed. Construction zones are marked with hazard symbols.

- Though most AccuTraffic city pages are not yet available, this site is worth checking periodically to see if the traffic report for the city you want has gone live.

Track Shipments

◆ UPS ◆ FedEx ◆ Other Sites

Track your business's shipments using shipping company Web sites. Both of the world's top package shipping companies, Federal Express and UPS, have very useful sites that can help you decide the most cost-effective way to send packages, track packages, and even prepare and print shipping forms using your computer and laser printer.

UPS

http://www.ups.com

 Complete shipping rate information and detailed drop-off site locator which includes site addresses, maps, and directions.

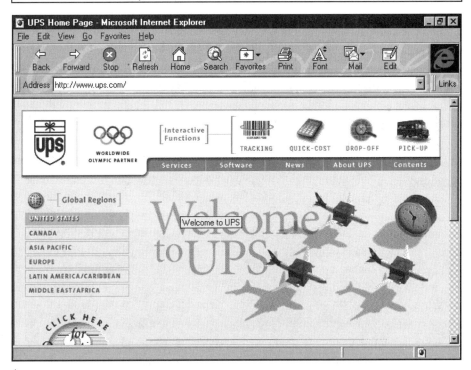

■ The UPS Web site is simple and well organized—you can get to any of the most commonly used features with one click via the Interactive Functions icons. Click Tracking, enter a package tracking number, and then click Track to find the location of a package. Click Quick Cost and enter the requested delivery and package information to find out the cost of shipping a package via a particular service. A list of costs for other UPS services is also supplied so that you can decide whether the extra cost of getting the package to its destination faster is worthwhile.

- Click Drop-Off to find the UPS drop-off locations nearest you. Enter the location you want to check and then click Search Locations. A map showing your location and the five nearest drop-off sites will appear. You can include self-service sites, staffed sites, or both in your location search.

- Click Pick-Up to schedule a UPS package pickup. The UPS site even has an icon for updated information on the status of ongoing UPS labor negotiations.

FedEx

http://www.fedex.com

 A quick way to open an account with FedEx, track packages, get rate information, and prepare a package for shipment.

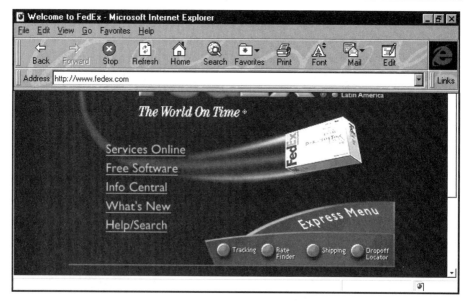

- This well-organized site lets you turn your computer into a full-fledged shipping station. Use the home page's Express Menu to jump to pages for tracking packages, finding rates (very important now that FedEx has moved to zone-based shipping charges), preparing packages for shipping, and finding the nearest drop-off location.

- Though finding a drop-off location is important if you're on the road and need to find a drop box fast, the Dropoff Locator merely states that there are over 40,000 convenient locations to drop off a package. It does, however, list partner businesses such as Kinko's and OfficeMax where FedEx drop boxes are located. So, if you know where a store for one of the partner businesses on the list is, you're in luck. You can also use supplied links to jump to the Web sites for these associated businesses.

- The Tracking service is easy to use. Just enter the airbill number for the package you want to track and the destination country, then click and let the software do the work. You can also use Advanced Tracking if you know the account to which number the package was billed.

- Perhaps the most useful service on the FedEx site is the InterNetShip page, which enables you to prepare a package airbill and print it, complete with a FedEx barcode, using your computer and laser printer. Simply enter your FedEx account number and a net User ID which you can obtain from the site, then enter the shipping and addressee information and print your airbill. You can also request a pickup from this part of the site and notify the recipient that you are sending the package via e-mail.

Other Sites

United States Postal Service

http://www.usps.com

- Track express packages, send the postal service change of address information, link to apply for a U.S. passport, calculate postage, and locate the nearest post office to a location.

DHL

http://www.dhl.com

- This site allows you to track DHL express packages using Airwaybill numbers, but it doesn't offer much in the way of other online services.

Hire Employees or Find a Job

◆ **The Monster Board** ◆ **Virtual Job Fair**
◆ **America's Job Bank** ◆ **Other Sites**

Avoid the high cost of hiring with recruiters by checking these Web sites. Most of these sites offer databases of resumes submitted by those seeking jobs. You can search these databases after registering with the site and/or paying a small fee. If you're looking for a career change, you can search the extensive databases of job openings at these sites free of charge. Also check into career planning resources and links to employer Web pages available at most of these sites.

The Monster Board

http://www.monsterboard.com

 Premier full-service job search and recruitment Web site offers career development and search agent services.

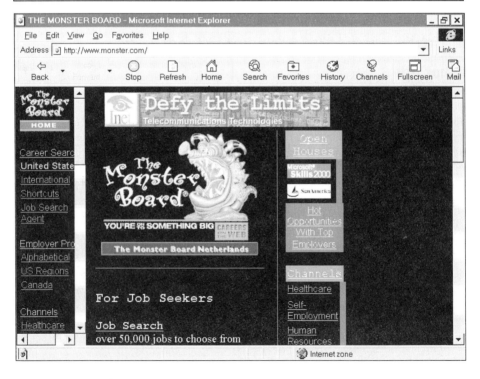

- Use The Monster Board to find your next star employee or find the next spot on your hike up the career ladder.

- Click the Career Search link to start looking for a job. On the Career Search Welcome page you can choose either a U.S. or International search of more than 8,500 total employers. Click the Personal Job Search Agent link to launch Swoop, a character in keeping with the monster site theme, who will zero in on job listings that fit a personal search profile you create.

- You can also click on Shortcut job search links such as healthcare, human resources, entry level, internship opportunities, and outdoor work.

- Click the Employer Profiles link to see an index of online company information brochures.

- Click the Career Center link to use the resume builder tool, check listings of upcoming hiring events, browse articles, get career advice, and check apartment and relocation listings.

- If you're looking for employees, click the Recruiters Center link. At the Recruiters Center you can search the Monster database of more than 200,000 resumes, use a resume search agent called 'Cruiter, or post a job on the site.

Virtual Job Fair

http://www.vjf.com/pub/jobsearch.html

 Top site for finding a job or hiring employees in the high-tech industries.

- Westech's Virtual Job Fair is designed to serve job seekers and employers in high-tech industries. Technical professionals will find that the Westech service yields superior results because it is targeted to high-tech companies.
- Westech sponsors ongoing job fairs in cities across the country and provides information about upcoming fairs at the Web site.
- Westech also publishes High Technology Careers Magazine, which you can access online by clicking the High Tech Careers icon. Here you can browse magazine articles and columns as well as search the alphabetical Employer's Directory.
- Click on the Job Search icon to enter search criteria for the Westech high-tech job database. This is a high-traffic site and should yield good results if you're looking for a high-tech job—more than 250,000 job search queries are processed by the Web site each day.

- Go to the Resume Center to submit your resume to the Virtual Job Fair. You can post resumes either in a public or private area of the site. Employers must register to search the resume database.

America's Job Bank

http://www.ajb.dni.us/index.html

 Post job openings free of charge on this site produced by a network of state employment agencies. Easy-to-use job search tools make this site well worthwhile.

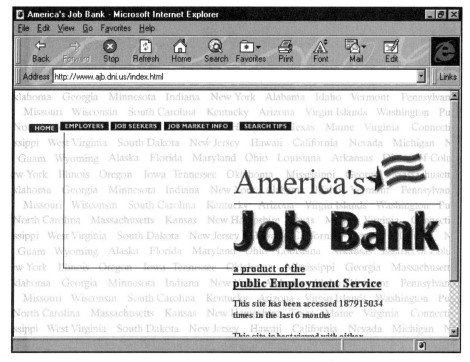

- Now you can put all of those unemployment insurance tax dollars to work for you by using the America's Job Bank Web site. This site is produced by the public Employment Service, a network of state employment agencies across the country.

- While not quite as feature-rich as other job search Web sites, all the basics are here, and employers can post job openings on the site free of charge. The site is funded by state unemployment insurance taxes.

- To post a job, click on the Employers link at the home page. You must fill out a brief registration form to use the employers service, but after doing so you can post jobs, link your Web site to the America's Job Bank site, use recruiting services, and use an automatic job posting service.

- If you're looking for a job, click on the Job Seekers link from the home page. The search tools at this site are easy to use and you can search using either a drop-down list of occupations and locations, a keyword search, or federal and military job codes. Click on the Employers Sites link to see an alphabetical index of more than 2,000 company Web pages.

- Click on the Job Market Info link to see career development information, including geographic profiles of state demographics, job search resources, and an interesting list of career trends showing what jobs and fields are expected to grow in the next ten years.

Other Sites

CareerPath.com

http://career.careerpath.com

- Founded and backed by six major newspapers, this site offers job hunters more than 150,000 positions no older than two weeks, gathered from employers' Web sites and the want ads of 45 newspapers across the country.

Online Career Center

http://www.occ.com

- This award-winning site was the first job clearinghouse page on the Web. Excellent career resources and easy-to-use job database searching make this site worth visiting.

E-Span

http://www.espan.com

- This site provides more in-depth screening services for both employers and job seekers to ensure that the right person is matched to the right job. There are fewer job listings here than at other sites, but greater selectivity in the screening process means a better chance of finding what you want.

Cut Phone and E-Mail Costs

◆ TRAC ◆ VDOPhone ◆ Yahoo! Mail ◆ JFAX ◆ Other Sites

Internet technology can help you cut your phone and e-mail costs in several ways. The sites listed here let you compare long-distance phone service prices, make long-distance calls over the Web, use free e-mail service, and get all your voice mail and faxes at one local phone number.

TRAC

http://www.trac.org

 Comparison-shop for the best long-distance plan to meet your calling profile.

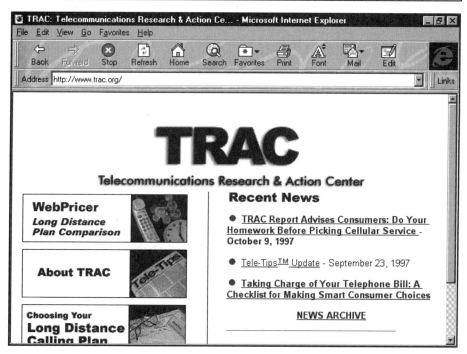

- TRAC, the Telecommunications Research & Action Center, is a non-profit organization with the stated mission of helping residential telecommunications customers. The TRAC Web site offers some excellent tools for making sure you get the best deal on long-distance telephone service.

- The primary benefit at the TRAC site is the WebPricer Long Distance Plan Comparison. The WebPricer allows you to compare five major long distance carriers (AT&T, MCI, Sprint, LCI, and Matrix) based on calling patterns you enter.

- Use the plan comparison form to enter how much you spend on long distance calling each month, your area code and three-number prefix, as well as the interstate numbers you want to compare (including the time of day you call). Note that the WebPricer does not compare long distance calls within your state.

- Comparison results are displayed in an easy-to-read dialog box, with calling plans listed from the lowest rate to the highest. Special promotion plans are also noted in the comparison results.

- At the TRAC home page, click on Choosing Your Long Distance Calling Plan to read helpful advice about topics such as Top Ways to Save Money on Your Long Distance Bill, Time Periods, and Telephone "Slamming."

VDOPhone

http://www.vdo.net

 Make free long distance phone calls over the Internet with VDOPhone. Trial version software also includes five hours of videophone calling over the Web.

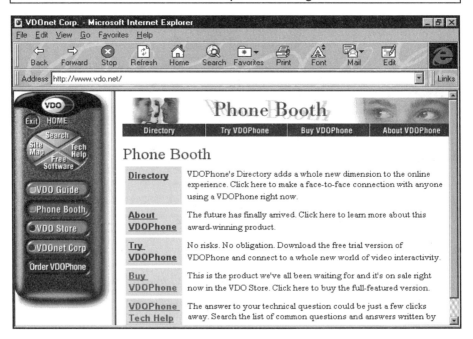

- VDO Corporation is the leading provider of video technology for the Internet. It has won several awards for both its products and its Web site. (See Appendix A for information on the free version of VDOLive video player software for the Web.)

- With VDOPhone, you can make long distance phone calls over the Internet, free of any long distance carrier charges, and you can use video capability to view another phone caller (who must also have VDOPhone installed) live on your computer.

- You can download a trial version of VDOPhone from this site by clicking Phone Booth on the remote control graphic at the left of the home page. Then click on the Try VDOPhone link to download the trial software.

- The free VDOPhone trial version has the same features and functions as the regular version, but the video capability of the trial version expires after 5 hours of use. You can search a directory of VDOPhone users who have the software and who can chat with you using video capability.

Yahoo! Mail

http://www.yahoo.com

 Log on to Yahoo! mail to get your e-mail over the Web free of charge. Consolidate your e-mail accounts into one service and get your e-mail from anywhere in the world.

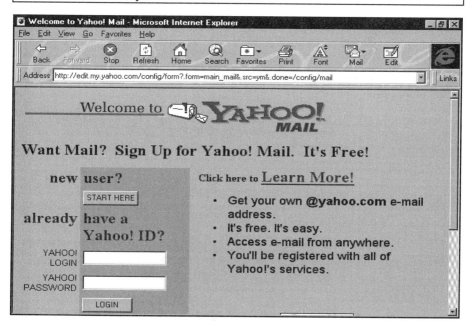

- Now here's a good idea: consolidate all your various e-mail accounts into one free account that you can access on the most popular Web directory site. That's the idea and here's the name—Yahoo! Mail.

- One of many free e-mail services now available on the Web, Yahoo! Mail is attractive not only because it's free, but because it's hosted by a site you probably visit a lot anyway. You can stop in at Yahoo! to search for information and then get your mail while you're at it. In addition, by getting a Yahoo! Mail account, you automatically register for all of Yahoo!'s other services.

- Another chief advantage of having a Yahoo! Mail account is the ability to log on from anywhere in the world using any computer to get your e-mail. You also avoid the hassle involved in setting up most dedicated e-mail services on your own computer.

- This is one of the truly great time and money savers on the Web today.

JFAX

http://www.jfax.com

 Route all your incoming faxes and voice mail to your e-mail inbox. Set up virtual offices in distant cities by using JFAX with local phone lines.

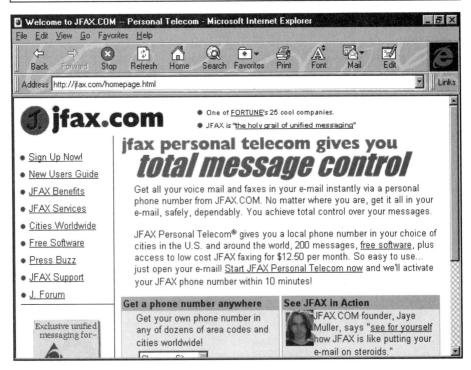

- Did you ever miss an important voice mail message because you were away from your phone? Did you ever miss a fax because the machine was out of paper or the line was busy? Have you ever experienced the hassle of sending and receiving faxes from your hotel and wondered why there wasn't a better way to do it?

- There is a better way. JFAX combines your voice mail and fax line into a local phone number in any city of your choice on the JFAX network. Voice mail and received faxes from this phone number are then sent to your e-mail inbox for you to read.

- You can set up local phone numbers in as many cities as you like or on a U.S. 1-800 phone number, thereby creating virtual offices where you can receive local phone calls and faxes.

- JFAX service is available in 29 cities, including seven outside the U.S. Each JFAX number costs as little as a long-distance phone call to some of these cities. The savings you achieve in paper and fax machine maintenance alone is worth the price of admission.

- With JFAX Send service you can send outgoing faxes over the Internet to any fax machine in the world. A new service called JFAX Notify! will page you whenever you receive an important fax or voice mail message. JFAX is perfect for sales reps, small business owners, and entrepreneurs who want to extend their presence at a low cost.

Other Sites

- There are several other sites that offer free e-mail service. At each site, the basic idea is the same: log on from any computer anywhere in the world and get your e-mail for free. The Pathfinder service offers free service as well as the choice of a unique specialty e-mail name for $14.95 per year.

MailExcite

http://mail.excite.com/

Pathfinder

http://pathfinder.mail.com

Buy Computer Hardware and Software

◆ **PC Magazine Online** ◆ **Internet Shopping Network** ◆ **Other Sites**

It stands to reason that the Internet is a great place to search for and purchase computer equipment. The number of technology-oriented Web sites makes finding bargains easy, and the advent of simple and secure online shopping sites means you can buy it better on the Net than at your local consumer electronics megastore.

PC Magazine Online

http://www.zdnet.com/pcmag/pcmag.htm

 Start your search for great computer hardware and software deals with this very comprehensive technology site.

- There are dozens of sites on the Web where you can search for deals on computer hardware and software, but perhaps the most

212

complete resource for your search is the PC Magazine Online Web site produced by Ziff-Davis as part of its ZDNet site.

- The PC Magazine site is a comprehensive resource for researching and making your next computer purchase. This site has the best selection of new product reviews, price comparison search engines, software downloads, and top feature columnists who can advise you about computer and technology trends.

- To make an educated purchasing decision, click the PC Labs Reviews icon or one of the specific hardware or software review category links underneath it. You can also click on the PC Magazine Editors' Choice Award Winners icon to read the editors' picks for best software and hardware.

- Click on the First Looks icon or one of the specific product links underneath it to read about the latest hardware and software to hit the market. Here you will find product reviews of the most cutting-edge computer products.

- The Trends link on the PC Magazine home page keeps you up to date on computer technology, with articles such as "Who's Winning the Browser Wars" and "What About Windows 98." The PC Tech link provides hands-on information for keeping your equipment on the cutting edge, and the Opinions link is where you will find columns from computer industry pundits such as John C. Dvorak.

- These are just a few of the tools available to help you in your initial product research, but there are a number of other, even more powerful tools to help you perform specific product feature and price comparisons.

- Click on the Products Channel for thousands of detailed product evaluations. The InternetUser provides development resources and how-to information for anyone who wants to use and build a Web site.

- The centerpiece of the buying experience at PC Magazine is NetBuyer. Click on the NetBuyer link to shop, compare, and buy hardware and software. Use the search engine to search by product category for the best deals. You can search either by product or by reviews. Click Specials to find hot deals or click on Basement for deals on overstocked or refurbished computers.

- After you find a price on equipment or software you want, it's always wise to check other sites to see if you can find a better deal. Even so, PC Magazine Online is certainly one of the best sites to use in making sure you get a great value.

Internet Shopping Network

http://www.internet.net

 The same people who produce the cable television Home Shopping Network run this excellent Computer Superstore shopping site.

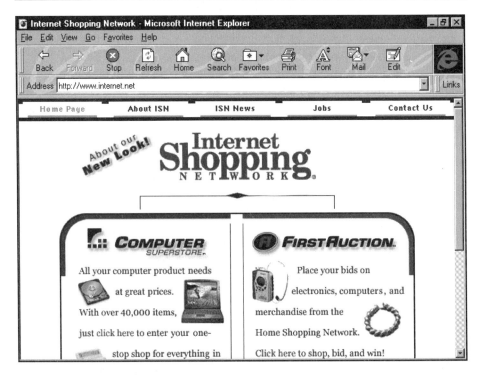

- Internet Shopping Network (ISN) is a great place to double-check prices against other shopping sites.

- Internet Shopping Network is a subsidiary of the cable television Home Shopping Network and was one of the first online shopping sites in the world. This pedigree of electronic shopping service helps make Internet Shopping Network an outstanding resource for getting the best deals available.

- Internet Shopping Network features two ways to buy: Computer Superstore and First Auction. Click Computer Superstore to shop an electronic database of more than 40,000 items.

- Once you're in the Computer Superstore, type a product name into the Product Search text box to find information on what you seek to buy. Click on Hot Deals Central to see featured bargains.

- Making a purchase at this site is easy. View information about a product and, if you like it, click Add to Bag. The item will appear in your virtual shopping bag. Then click either Buy Now to proceed to a credit card information entry form or click Continue Shopping. You can also click Empty Bag if you change your mind.

- If you want to try a different way to buy, click on the First Auction side of the ISN home page. This part of the site features all types of items shown on the cable Home Shopping Network, not only computer products.

Other Sites

Software.net

http://www.software.net

- Software.net specializes in software you can buy and download all at one simple, secure site. More than 3,000 titles are available for immediate purchase and download, and more than 29,000 titles are included in the complete catalog for purchase. If you don't want to download a software purchase, you can have it shipped in the traditional shrink-wrapped box.

Insight Direct

http://www.insight.com

- Listed as one of Fortune's 25 "cool companies," Insight Direct offers great technical support, installation advice, and an easy-to-use interface for finding computer bargains. A search engine text box on the home page makes it easy to find a specific item quickly, and the Outrageous Deals feature e-mails you updates on limited time deals that often prove to be outstanding values.

PCWorld Online

http://www.pcworld.com

- PCWorld Online is another fine site for in-depth analysis of computer hardware and software products, similar to the PC Magazine Online site. Check here for an update on computer tech news, features, and columns from PC World magazine. Click the Top 400 Link for the top 400 software and hardware product reviews.

Troubleshoot Computer Problems

◆ ZDNet Help Channel ◆ Indiana University Knowledge Base
◆ Internet Help Desk ◆ Other Sites

What do you do when you receive the dreaded "not enough memory to perform operation" error message? How do you open a zip file? When you need answers to questions such as these, you can turn to the Web sites listed here. These sites provide detailed information that can help you troubleshoot computer hardware and software problems as well as find technical support at other Web sites.

ZDNet Help Channel

http://www.zdnet.com/zdhelp/hpc/

 Get help from the combined resources and expertise of publications such as PC Computing and PC Magazine at this top technology site.

- ZDNet is the online home of Ziff-Davis, the publisher of popular computer publications such as PC Magazine, PC Week, and PC

Computing. The site includes a great section called the Help! Channel that provides a front door to the combined resources and expertise of the Ziff-Davis magazines. Just click the URL noted on the previous page or go to the ZDNet home page and click on Help!

- At the Help! Channel page you can click icons to Fix It Now!, Find a Tip!, or access Downloads! (the site tends to get carried away with the exclamation points, but it's a minor irritant).

- Clicking Fix It Now! takes you to a search engine page where you can type in your question or problem and then search the ZDNet database of tips and answers for the solution. The database is extensive, so you will likely find some help here.

- If you can't find the help you need, click on the SupportFinder icon to see an alphabetical directory of vendor Web site links. Search for the maker of the hardware or software you're having trouble with and click to get help. If all else fails, you can also click the ServiceFinder icon to find the closest repair shop to you.

- If you want to test the performance of your computer while you're at the ZDNet site, click on the SpeedRate icon. Click the Video Demos link to access video demos for basic PC maintenance.

- You will find a wealth of other resources at the Help! Channel, including Frequently Asked Questions, Ask the Experts, and online users forums. And don't forget to check out other parts of the ZDNet site for computer and technology news, information, and resources.

Indiana University Knowledge Base

http://kb.indiana.edu/

 Take advantage of this extensive database of computer troubleshooting and instruction provided by a Big Ten university.

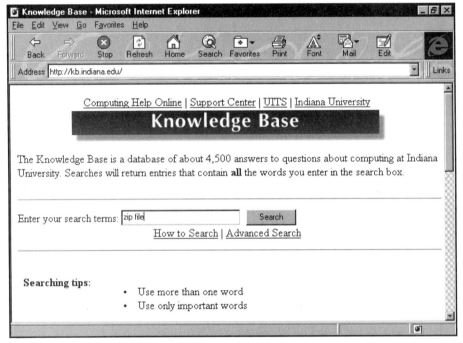

- Use the Indiana University Knowledge Base to answer questions you have about your computer. This Web site is maintained by a university campus computing center, and the breadth of information contained in its database includes more than 4,500 documents. This site is worth checking if you're having computer trouble or if you just want to learn more about a computing topic.

- Though you can search an index of common Knowledge Base topics by clicking on Menus, this list of links includes only a small portion of the available database.

- The best way to find an answer is to simply enter a topic or question. Avoid one-word and very specific searches for best results. Though some links and documents in the Knowledge Base pertain to the specifics of using computers on the Indiana University computing network, most files provide clear, concise general computing instructions or troubleshooting information.

- You can also click the Glossary link to see entries that provide definitions of computing terminology.

Internet Help Desk

http://w3.one.net/~alward/

 Find troubleshooting tips, links to tools, Web guides, consulting services, and more at this free service site.

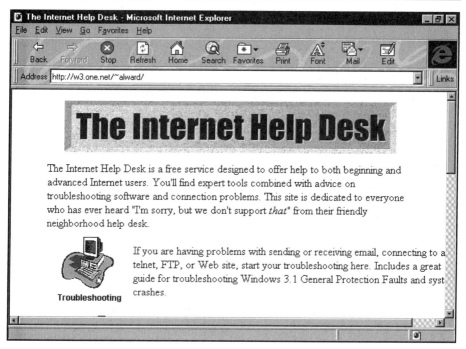

- The Internet Help Desk is a small site run by Amy L. Ward to, in her words, "meet my nerdish impulses," but it does provide some good links to Internet help.
- Click on the Troubleshooting icon to see charts that describe what to do when you receive e-mail, Netscape, Explorer, and FTP error messages.
- For example, imagine you have been receiving an "out of memory" error message when loading a Web page with Internet Explorer. Click the Explorer link and see that the cause may be that your machine's virtual memory may be disabled. The recommended remedy is to open your Control Panel and check the Virtual Memory system settings.
- The advice provided at this Web site is quick and easy to follow.

Other Sites

Computer Security Information

http://www.alw.nih.gov/Security/security.html

- This site provides a good overview of available security software and links to other security sites and information. This is a good place to start your search for information about security on the Web.

National Computer Security Association

http://www.ncsa.com/hotlinks/

- There is no shortage of security sites on the Web, but this is perhaps the best place to start your search for security software developers. Not as much information here compared to other security sites—links on this page are primarily to developer sites.

Appendix A: Essential Downloads

◆ Internet Explorer ◆ Netscape Navigator ◆ TUCOWS
◆ Shareware.Com ◆ The Jumbo Download Network
◆ VDOLive Video Player ◆ Adobe Acrobat Reader ◆ Shockwave

The Internet can be a convenient source for downloading valuable software. Log on to the following URLs to download Web and multimedia software, much of which is available free of charge or as shareware, which requires a minimal registration fee.

Internet Explorer

http://www.microsoft.com/ie/download/

- Internet Explorer 4.0 is the latest version of Microsoft's Internet browser software. It has attracted a lot of attention for both it's powerful new features and it's role in the Department of Justice investigation of Microsoft for antitrust violations.

- Explorer 4.0's active desktop features allow the browser software to be much more integrated into the Windows operating system you use to run your computer.

- You can also receive active content from the Web using Explorer's "push" technology. Active content lets you choose from among several Web content "channels" to receive automatic information updates to your desktop.

- Other Explorer 4.0 tools include NetMeeting virtual conferencing software and FrontPage Express. NetMeeting helps facilitate virtual meetings held via the Internet and one-to-one telephone calls from your computer. FrontPage Express enables you to create and post your own Web pages.

- Whatever the outcome of the legal wrangling, Explorer is rapidly gaining market acceptance as the leading Web browser. Get your copy free of charge at this site.

Netscape Navigator

http://home.netscape.com/download/index.html

- Netscape Navigator 4.0 is the other major Web browser on the market today and the direct descendant of the Mosaic browser that first swept many users into the world of surfing the Web.

- Netscape Communicator includes Navigator 4.0 and a complete suite of Internet tools, including Messenger for e-mail, Collabra for newsgroups, and Composer for creating Web pages.

- You can also download a complete installation of Netscape Communicator which includes Netscape Netcaster for receiving active channel content, Netscape Conference for online collaboration and the capability to handle rich multimedia content as well as bitstream fonts.

- Though you must pay for Netscape products available at this download site, you can download evaluation versions of new software free of charge. Educational institutions and nonprofit organizations can download a number of Netscape products at no charge.

TUCOWS

http://www.tucows.com

- TUCOWS stands for The Ultimate Collection Of Winsock Software. The site bills itself as the world's best collection of Internet software.

- After logging on to the TUCOWS home page, click the appropriate link for your geographical location (such as United States, Europe, Canada), then click the appropriate state (or other area) link. These geographical links are used to produce faster and more reliable software downloads.

- Next click the appropriate link for your computer's operating system. You will see a directory page listing links for more than 60 different types of Internet software.

- Click on a category link to see a listing of software available in that category for downloading. Listings include a complete description of the software, its hardware requirements, and a rating of the software (by number of cows). Click the Download button next to a particular listing to start downloading.

- Most software available at TUCOWS is either shareware or freeware, though some products offered are only demo versions that may have limited features or time restraints.

Shareware.Com

http://www.shareware.com

- Shareware.Com is another great site for downloading software via the Web. The site is a service of the C/Net Web page, noted for its computer and technology news coverage.

- You can browse the site by clicking on the New Arrivals or Most Popular links, or you can simply enter the name of the software you hope to find in the search engine text box.

- Highlights of available shareware are shown on the home page. Click on a link to go to a description of the shareware and a link to the download page.

The Jumbo Download Network

http://www.jumbo.com

- Yet another great software downloading site is The Jumbo Download Network, which lists more than 250,000 shareware programs and links. Available software is conveniently organized by channels, including Business, Desktop, Internet, Utilities, Games, Entertainment, Developer, and Demo City, which offers the latest commercial demos so you can try before you buy.

VDOLive Video Player

http://www.vdo.net/download/

- Download VDOnet Corporation's VDOLive Video Player 3.0 free of charge at this site. VDOLive is the top software for broadcasting and receiving video content over the Internet and is used by many major television networks, including CBS News, MTV, and PBS.

- Click on the VDOLive 3.0 link to begin downloading the software. You must register to download, but otherwise the procedure is free and relatively easy. Only the VDOLive Player software is available for free download. VDOLive server software must be purchased.

- You can also download a trial version of VDOPhone, touted as the first full-color video telephone available for either regular telephone lines or the Internet. VDOPhone lets you see and hear anyone over the Internet with no additional phone charges.

- VDOPhone is currently available for Windows 95 users only. The trial version expires after 5 hours of video reception.

Adobe Acrobat Reader

http://www.adobe.com

- Adobe Acrobat Reader lets you view, navigate, and print many document files available on the Web for downloading.

- To download the Acrobat Reader free of charge, click the Free Plug-Ins and Updates link at the Adobe home page. The link takes you to a file library page that displays a list of nearly thirty software products you can download. Links to download sites for each type of software are displayed by operating system.

- Click the Acrobat Reader link for your computer's operating system. The reader is available for Windows, Macintosh, DOS, UNIX, and OS/2. You will go to a page including short description links and download links for the available versions of Acrobat Reader. Click the Download link to register and begin downloading.

- You can also click the Tryout Software link at the Adobe home page to see descriptions of Adobe's latest multimedia and graphics products as well as download links for trial versions.

Shockwave

http://www.macromedia.com/shockwave/download/

- Macromedia Shockwave facilitates smooth viewing of animation and multimedia over the Internet. Many Web browsers and online services such as Internet Explorer, Netscape Navigator, and AOL include Shockwave with their software.

- If you want to download Shockwave, go to the Shockwave Download Center at the above URL, and click the Get Shockwave link.

Appendix B: Timesaving Tools

◆ Financial Calculators ◆ Calculators Online
◆ Universal Currency Converter ◆ The Time Zones Page ◆ Naval Clock
◆ Fast Area Code Finder ◆ National Address and Zip+4 Browser

Use the Web tools listed here to save time by finding the answer to many common financial and mathematical questions. You can also get the correct time around the world with the Time Zones and Naval Clock sites.

Financial Calculators

http://www.moneyadvisor.com/calc/

- Have you ever wondered whether you should lease or purchase a car? How much money do you have to save to become a millionaire by the time you retire? How much rent can you afford?

- The financial calculators available at the Financial Calculators page of the TimeValue Software Web site provide a host of interesting and practical tools for finding the answer to your financial questions.

- The directory of calculator links includes categories such as Auto Loans & Leasing, Loans & Savings Calculators, General Financial Calculators, Mortgage Calculators, Insurance Calculators, Tax Calculators, and Just For Fun Calculators.

Calculators Online

http://www-sci.lib.uci.edu/HSG/RefCalculators.html

- Another calculator site at Martindale's "The Reference Desk" provides more than 5,300 calculators.

- Links to the calculators are arranged in an alphabetical index of categories and subtopics. Click on a link to use one of the calculators.

- Business categories include Home & Office, Finance, Management/Business, Insurance, Stocks, Bonds, Options, and Commodities & Futures.

- You can also find many calculators for practical matters such as clothing, arts and crafts, medical, and law. Numerous mathematics and science calculators are also available, from simple unit conversion calculators to astrophysics.

Universal Currency Converter

http://www.xe.net./currency/

- This simple and useful Web site does one thing only, but does it well—currency conversion. If, for example, you want to know how many French francs you can get for $100, turn to this Web page.
- Type the amount of currency you want to convert, then select the type of currency (e.g., U.S. dollars). Next, select the type of currency you're converting to (e.g., French francs), and click the Perform Currency Conversion button.
- The Currency Converter tells you that $100 converts to 596.90 French francs. (Note that currency exchange rates fluctuate and converting currency usually requires a fee.)

The Time Zone Page

http://www.west.net/~lindley/zone/

- Another simple but very useful site is the Time Zone Page. Find the current time for more than 600 cities around the world.
- Select a city from the menu, then click Get the Time!

Naval Clock

http://tycho.usno.navy.mil/cgi-bin/timer.pl

- To check the most accurate clock available, go to the Naval Clock Web site. The site displays the current time in all North American time zones as well as Universal Time (also called Greenwich Mean Time).

Fast Area Code Finder

http://www.555-1212.com/aclookup.html

- Find an area code fast at this handy site. Simply enter a city name and/or click on a state from the drop-down list menu, then click Get Area Code! If you know the area code but want to find where the code serves, type the area code in the Area Code text box and click Get Location.

National Address and ZIP+4 Browser

http://www.semaphorecorp.com/cgi/form.html

- If you need to look up a Zip Code, go to this site and enter the company name plus as much of its address as you know. The Zip Browser returns the complete, correct address, including the correct 9-digit Zip Code. Great for cleaning up old mailing lists.

Appendix C: Viruses

Introduction

- Viruses are malicious programs written to attempt some form of deliberate destruction to someone's computer. They are instructions or code that have been written to reproduce as they attach themselves to other programs without the user's knowledge. Viruses can be programmed to do anything a computer can do. Viruses are a nuisance, but if you know how they work and take the necessary precautions to deal with them, they are manageable. It is essential that you understand the nature of these programs, how they work, and how they can be disinfected. No one is exempt from viruses; strict precautions and anti-virus programs are the answer.

- Viruses are potentially destructive to one file or to an entire hard disk, whether the file or hard disk is one used in a standalone computer or in a multi-user network. Like biological viruses, computer viruses need a host, or a program, to infect. Once infection has been transferred, the viruses can spread like wildfire through the entire library of files. Like human sickness, viruses come in many different forms; some are more debilitating than others.

Origins of Viruses

- How do you get a virus? They can come from a couple of places:
  - An infected diskette
  - Downloading an infected file from a bulletin board, the Internet, or an online service
- Knowing where viruses are likely to be introduced will make you sensitive to the possibility of getting one.

Categories of Viruses

- Viruses come in two categories:
  - Boot Sector Viruses
  - File Viruses
- **Boot Sector Viruses** may also be called System Sector viruses because they attack the system sector. System or boot sectors contain programs that are executed when the PC is booted. System or boot sectors do not have files. The hardware reads information in the area in the bootup sections of the computer. Because these sectors are vital for PC operation, they are prime target areas for viruses.
- Two types of system sectors exist: DOS sectors and partition sectors. PCs characteristically have a DOS sector and one or more sectors created by the partitioning command, FDISK, or proprietary partitioning software. Partition sectors are commonly called Master Boot Records (MBR). Viruses that attach to these areas are seriously damaging ones.
- **File Viruses** are more commonly found. Characteristically, a file virus infects by overwriting part or all of a file.

Timing of Viruses

- Viruses come in many sizes and with various symptoms. For example, a virus may attach itself to a program immediately and begin to infect an entire hard disk. Or the virus can be written to attack at a specific time. For example, the Michelangelo virus strikes on his birthday each May.
- Some viruses are written so that they delay letting you know of their existence until they have done major damage.

Virus Symptoms

- How can you tell if you have a virus? Hopefully, you will install anti-virus software in your PC that will identify viruses and make you aware immediately upon entry to your system. Otherwise, you may experience different symptoms such as:
  - Slow processing
  - Animation or sound appearing out of nowhere
  - Unusually heavy disk activity
  - Odd changes in files
  - Unusual printer activity

Precautions

- Most viruses spread when you have booted the computer from an infected diskette. A healthy precaution here would be to boot only from the hard drive.

    - Backup all files. At least two complete backups are recommended.

    - Even new software can come with a virus; scan every diskette before use.

    - Mark all software program attributes as read only.

    - Research and update anti-virus products on an ongoing basis to have the latest protection.

    - Since there are many types of viruses, one type of anti-virus protection won't disinfect all viruses. The safest approach is to install a multiple anti-virus program library.

Appendix D: Emoticons and Abbreviations

Since you cannot see the people with whom you communicate on the Internet, here are some symbols you can use to convey emotion in your messages. This section also contains some acronyms that you will encounter in Internet messages (such as e-mail, newsgroup messages, and chat room discussions). Be sure to use these cute symbols and abbreviations *only* in your personal communications.

For more emoticons and acronyms, go to the Emoticons & Smileys page:

http://home.earthlink.net/~gripweeds/emoticon.htm

Emoticons

- Use these symbols to convey emotions in your messages. To see the faces in these symbols, turn the page to the right.

>:->	Angry	:-(	Sad
5:-)	Elvis	:-@	Scream
:-)	Happy	:-#	Secret (lips are sealed)
()	Hug	:P	Sticking Tongue Out
:-D	Joking	:-O	Surprised
:*	Kiss	:-J	Tongue in Cheek
:/)	Not Funny	;-)	Wink

Acronyms

- Listed below are some of the more-common acronyms, but new acronyms are always being created. Be sure to check online to see what's new.

ADN	Any day now	**GMTA**	Great minds think alike
ASAP	As soon as possible	**IAE**	In any event
B4N	Bye for now	**IMO**	In my opinion
BRB	Be right back	**IRL**	In real life
BTW	By the way	**JIC**	Just in case
DTRT	Do the right thing	**LOL**	Laugh out loud
F2F	Face to face	**ROTFL**	Rolling on the floor laughing
FAQ	Frequently asked questions	**RTM**	Read the manual
FWIW	For what it's worth	**TIA**	Thanks in advance
FYI	For your information	**WFM**	Works for me

Appendix E: Netiquette

Netiquette is the art of civilized communications between people on the Internet. Whenever you send an e-mail message, a chat room message, or a newsgroup message follow these guidelines.

A Few Tips

- Always include a subject in the message heading. This makes it easy for the recipient to organize messages in folders by topic and to find a message by browsing through message headers.

- Do not use capital letters. To the recipient, it feels like YOU ARE SHOUTING. Instead, enclose text that you want to emphasize with asterisks. For example: I *meant* Friday of *next* week.

- Be careful with the tone you use. With the absence of inflection, it is easy to send a message that can be misinterpreted by the recipient. Use emoticons to establish your intent. A smiley emoticon can make it clear to the recipient that you are really joking.

- Spell check your messages before you send them. They represent you.

- Do not send flame messages. These are obnoxious, offensive, or otherwise disturbing messages. If you send this type of message to a newsgroup, 30,000 people who read your flame will think less of you. If you receive flame mail, probably the best thing you can do is press the Delete button rather than the Reply button.

- Messages sent over the Internet are not private. Your message is in writing and nothing can prevent someone from forwarding it to anyone they please. Assume that anyone with a computer has the potential to read your message.

- Never initiate or forward a chain letter. Some service providers will cancel your membership if you do so, as they are trying to protect their members from unwanted mail.

- If you send a long message, it is a good idea to tell the recipient at the beginning of the message so that they can decide if they would rather download it to read later.

The Netiquette Home Page
http://www.albion.com/netiquette/index.html

- This page lists hyperlinks to pages on Netiquette contributed by Internet users. You will find interesting, amusing, and very important material in these sites.

Glossary

Listed below and on the following pages are terms that you may encounter on your Internet travels.

address book A place where frequently used e-mail addresses are stored.

anonymous FTP A special kind of FTP service that allows any user to log on. Anonymous FTP sites have a predefined user named "anonymous" that accepts any password.

Archie A database system of FTP resources. It helps you find files that exist anywhere on the Internet.

ARPAnet (Advanced Research Projects Administration Network) Ancestor to the Internet: ARPAnet began in 1969 as a project developed by the US Department of Defense. Its initial purpose was to enable researchers and military personnel to communicate in the event of an emergency.

ASCII file (American Standard Code for Information Interchange) File containing ASCII-formatted text only; can be read by almost any computer or program in the world.

attachment File(s) or Web pages(s) enclosed with an e-mail message.

Base64 (MIME) encoding One of the encoding schemes, used in the MIME (Multipurpose Internet Mail Extensions) protocol.

binary file A file containing machine language (that is, ones and zeros) to indicate that the file is more than plain text. A binary file must be encoded (converted to ASCII format) before it can be passed through the e-mail system.

BinHex An encoding scheme for the Macintosh platform that allows a file to be read as text when passed through the e-mail system.

bookmark A browser feature that memorizes and stores the path to a certain Web site. Creating bookmarks enables a quick return to favorite sites.

browser A graphic interface program that helps manage the process of locating information on the World Wide Web. Browser programs such as Netscape Navigator and Microsoft Internet Explorer provide simple searching techniques and create paths that can return you to sites you visited previously.

chat (Internet Relay Chat) A live "talk" session with other Internet or network users in which a conversation is exchanged back and forth.

Glossary

client program A computer program designed to talk to a specific server program. The FTP client program is designed to ask for and use the FTP service offered by an FTP server program. Client programs usually run in your own computer, and talk to server programs in the computers it connects to.

client A computer that is signing onto another computer. The computer that is logging on acts as the client; the other computer acts as the server.

complex search Uses two or more words in a text string (and may also use operators that modify the search string) to search for matches in a search engine's catalog.

compressed file A file that has been made smaller (without lost data) by using a file compression program such as pkzip or StuffIt. Compressed files are easier to send across the Internet, as they take less time to upload and download.

copyright The legal right of ownership of published material. E-mail messages are covered by copyright laws. In most cases, the copyright owner is the writer of the message.

crawlers Another name for search engines.

directories Also referred to as folders. Directories are lists of files and other directories. They are used for organizing and storing computer files.

domain The portion of an Internet address that follows the @ symbol and identifies the computer you are logging onto.

downloading Copying files (e-mail, software, documents, etc.) from a remote computer to your own computer.

e-mail (electronic mail) A communication system for exchanging messages and attached files. E-mail can be sent to anyone in the world as long as both parties have access to the Internet and an Internet address to identify themselves.

encoding A method of converting a binary file to ASCII format for e-mail purposes. Common encoding schemes include Uuencoding and MIME (Base64) encoding.

fair use The right to use short quotes and excerpts from copyrighted material such as e-mail messages.

FAQ (Frequently Asked Questions document) A text document that contains a collection of frequently asked questions about a particular subject. FAQs on many subjects are commonly available on the Web.

file "File" is a general term usually used to describe a computer document. It may also be used to refer to more than one file, however, such as groups of documents, software, games, etc.

folders/ directories Folders, also referred to as directories, are organized storage areas for maintaining computer files. Like filing cabinets, they help you manage your documents and files.

font A typeface that contains particular style and size specifications.

freeware Software that can be used for free forever. No license is required and the software may be copied and distributed legally.

FTP (File Transfer Protocol) The method of remotely transferring files from one computer to another over a network (or across the Internet). It requires that both the client and server computers use special communication software to talk to one another.

FTP site An Internet site that uses File Transfer Protocol and enables files to be downloaded and/or uploaded. When you access an FTP site through a browser application, however, your log-in is considered "anonymous" and will not allow uploading.

FTP (File Transfer Protocol) A computer program used to move files from one computer to another. The FTP program usually comes in two parts: a server program that runs in the computers offering the FTP service, and a client program running in computers, like yours, that wish to use the service.

Gopher A menu system that allows you to search various sources available on the Internet. It is a browsing system that works much like a directory or folder. Each entry may contain files and/or more directories to dig through.

heading fields (headings) Individual fields, like To and From, in the header of an e-mail message.

hierarchically structured catalog A catalog of Web sites that is organized into a few major categories that have sub-categories under them. Each sub-category has additional sub-categories under it. The level of detail in this structure depends on the particular Web site.

home page A Web site's starting point. A home page is like a table of contents. It outlines what a particular site has to offer, and usually contains connecting links to other related areas of the Internet as well.

host A central computer that other computers log onto for the purpose of sharing and exchanging information.

hot lists Lists of Web sites that you have visited or "ear-marked" and wish to return to later. Your browser program will store the paths to those sites and generate a short-cut list for future reference.

HTML (HyperText Mark Up Language) The programming language used to create Web pages so that they can be viewed, read, and accessed from any computer running on any type of operating system.

HTTP (HyperText Transfer Protocol) The communication protocol that allows for Web pages to connect to one another, regardless of what type of operating system is used to display or access the files.

hypertext or hypermedia The system of developing clickable text and objects (pictures, sound, video, etc.) to create links to related documents or different sites on the Internet.

inbox Where incoming e-mail messages are stored and retrieved.

Information Superhighway Nickname for the Internet: a vast highway by which countless pieces of information are made available and exchanged back and forth among its many users.

Internet A world-wide computer network that connects several thousand businesses, schools, research foundations, individuals, and other networks. Anyone with access can log on, communicate via e-mail, and search for various types of information.

Internet address The user ID utilized by an individual or host computer on the Internet. An Internet address is usually associated with the ID used to send and receive e-mail. It consists of the user's ID followed by the domain.

Internet Protocol The method of communication which allows information to be exchanged across the Internet and across varying platforms that may be accessing or sending information.

ISP (Internet Service Providers) Private or public organizations that offer access to the Internet. Most charge a monthly or annual fee and generally offer such features as e-mail accounts, a pre-determined number of hours for Internet access time (or unlimited access for a higher rate), special interest groups, etc.

links Hypertext or hypermedia objects that, once selected, will connect you to related documents or other areas of interest.

login A process by which you gain access to a computer by giving it your username and password. If the computer doesn't recognize your login, access will be denied.

macro virus A virus written in the macro language of a particular program (such as Word) and contained in a program document. When the document is opened, the macro is executed, and the virus usually adds itself to other, similar documents. Macro virus can be only as destructive as the macro language allows.

message header The group of heading fields at the start of every e-mail program, used by the e-mail system to route and otherwise deal with your mail.

meta-tree structured catalog Another term for hierarchically structured catalog.

modem A piece of equipment (either internal or external) that allows a computer to connect to a phone line for the purpose of dialing into the Internet, another network, or an individual computer.

modem speed (baud rate) Indicates at what speed your computer will be able to communicate with a computer on the other end. The higher the rate, the quicker the response time for accessing files and Web pages, processing images, downloading software, etc.

multimedia The process of using various computer formats: pictures, text, sound, movies, etc.

multithread search engines Software that searches the Web sites of other search engines and gathers the results of these searches for your use.

netiquette (Network etiquette) The network equivalent of respectfulness and civility in dealing with people and organizations.

network A group of computers (two or more) that are connected to one another through various means, usually cable or dial-in connections.

newsgroup A bulletin board of news information. Users specify which news topic they are interested in, and subscribe to receive information on that topic.

newsreader A program that allows you to read and respond to Usenet newsgroups.

offline The process of performing certain tasks, such as preparing e-mail messages, prior to logging onto the Internet.

online The process of performing certain tasks, such as searching the Web or responding to e-mail, while actually logged onto the Internet.

online services Organizations that usually offer Internet access as well as other services, such as shareware, technical support, group discussions, and more. Most online services charge a monthly or annual fee.

operators Words or symbols that modify the search string instead of being part of it.

outbox Where offline e-mail messages are stored. The contents of an outbox are uploaded to the Internet once you log on and prompt your e-mail program to send them.

packet A body of information that is passed through the Internet. It contains the sender's and receiver's addresses and the item that is being sent. Internet Protocol is used to route and process the packet.

platform Refers to the type of computer and its corresponding operating system, such as PC, Macintosh, UNIX. The Internet is a multi-platform entity, meaning that all types of computers can access it.

POP (Post Office Protocol) The method used to transfer e-mail messages from your mail server to your system.

public domain freeware Software that can be used for free; usually the author is anonymous.

quote format A way of displaying text quoted from other e-mail messages, most frequently used in replies. Quoted text usually has a character like ">" at the start of each line. Some e-mail programs let you set the style of quoted material.

search engine A software program that goes out on the Web, seeks Web sites, and catalogs them – usually by downloading their home pages.

search sites Web sites that contain catalogs of Web resources that can be searched by headings, URLs, and key words.

self-extracting archive Macintosh-platform compressed file that does not require external software for decompression. These files usually end with an .sea extension.

self-extracting file PC-platform compressed file that does not require external software for decompression. These files usually end with an .exe extension.

server program A computer program that offers a service to other computer programs called client programs. The FTP server program offers the FTP service to FTP client programs. Server programs usually run in computers you will be connecting to.

server A computer that is accessed by other computers on a network. It usually shares files with or provides other services to the client computers that log onto it.

shareware Computer programs, utilities and other items (fonts, games, etc.) that can be downloaded or distributed free of charge, but with the understanding that if you wish to continue using it, you will send the suggested fee to the developer.

signature A few lines of text automatically appended to the body of an e-mail message. Signatures usually include the sender's address plus other information.

simple search Uses a text string, usually a single word, to search for matches in a search engine's catalog.

.sit file A Macintosh file compressed by using a compression application called StuffIt.

SLIP (Serial Line Internet Protocol) Software that allows for a direct serial connection to the Internet. SLIP allows your computer to become part of the Internet – not just a terminal accessing the Internet. If your computer is set up with SLIP, you can Telnet or FTP other computers directly without having to go through an Internet provider.

SMTP (Simple Mail Transfer Protocol) The method used to transfer e-mail messages between servers and from your system to your mail server.

spiders Another name for search engines.

standalone FTP client program A standalone computer program designed to talk to an FTP server program running at a remote computer site that offers FTP services. The FTP client program can ask for the files you want and send files you wish to deliver. The client program runs in your computer; the server program runs at the site.

start page The opening page within a browser application. This is the page from which all other Web site links are built. A browser's start page is its home page by default, but you can customize your browser to begin with any Web site as your start page.

subject-structured catalog A catalog organized under a few broad subject headings. The number and names of these headings depend on the Web site.

surfing the Internet Exploring various World Wide Web sites and links to search for information on the Internet. Using FTP, WAIS, and Gopher servers can further assist in the surfing/searching process – as can a good Internet browser.

TCP/IP (Transmission Control Protocol/ Internet Protocol) The communication system that is used between networks on the Internet. It checks to make sure that information is being correctly sent and received from one computer to another.

Telnet A program that allows one computer to log on to another host computer. This process allows you to use any of the features available on the host computer, including sharing data and software, participating in interactive discussions, etc.

text format file Same as the ASCII format file: a document that has been formatted to be read by almost any computer or program in the world.

text string A string of ASCII characters. The text string may or may not contain operators.

threaded messages Messages grouped so that replies to a message are grouped with the original message. When threaded messages are sorted, threads are kept together.

uploading The process of copying computer files (e-mail, software, documents, etc.) from one's own computer to a remote computer.

URL (Uniform Resource Locator) A locator command used only within the World Wide Web system to create or hunt for linked sites. It operates and looks much like an Internet Address.

Usenet A world-wide discussion system, operating on linked Usenet servers, consisting of a set of newsgroups where articles or messages are posted covering a variety of subjects and interests. You can use your browser or a newsreader program to access the newsgroups available from your Internet provider's Usenet server.

UUencoding One of the encoding schemes, short for UNIX-to-UNIX encoding. UUencoding is common on all platforms, not just UNIX.

virus A small, usually destructive computer program that hides inside innocent-looking programs. Once the virus is executed, it attaches itself to other programs. When triggered, often by the occurrence of a date or time on the computer's internal clock/calendar, it executes a nuisance or damaging function, such as printing a message or reformatting your hard disk.

WAIS (Wide Area Information Servers) A system that allows for searches for information based on actual contents of files, not just file titles.

Web robots Software which automatically searches the Web for new sites.

Web Site A location on the Internet that represents a particular company, organization, topic, etc. It normally contains links to more information within a site, as well as suggested links to related sites on the Internet.

World Wide Web (WWW) An easy-to-use system for finding information on the Internet through the use of hypertext or hypermedia linking. Hypertext and hypermedia consist of text and graphic objects that, when you click on them, automatically link you to different areas of a site or to related Internet sites.

zip file PC file compressed with pkzip. Zipped files usually need to be unzipped with pkunzip before they can be used.

Index

A

B

C

Index

Index

244

Notes

Notes

Notes